This is an exquisite book, an intelligent and thoughtful look into a woman's life that will reward any reader, not just those close to the Hudson Valley. Litterine masterfully combines words and images to present a vision that begins with the history of the river town where she grew up then spirals inward. Playing with the collapse of time, we are gifted with a keen perspective that ranges from the historical to the geographic to the personal and communal.

    Donna Baier Stein
    Author, *The Silver Baron's Wife*

This is a beautiful, moving, and sometimes heartbreaking account of what it was like to come of age in a working-class New Jersey town in the 1950's and 1960's. The writing is luminous and evocative, and the author's eye for detail is remarkable. You'll feel as if you're transported back to another era, to a world filled with both pain and delight.

    Constance Rosenblum
    Author, *Boulevard of Dreams: Heady Times, Heartbreak, and Hope Along the Grand Concourse in the Bronx*

Beautifully illustrated, it's a seamless mix of town and family history, vivid characters with their own points of view, and surprising revelations. With the river as the memoir's organizing principle, the reader floats through Litterine's life from girlhood to womanhood in a working-class town across from Manhattan, a town which changes so completely, it's now called the Gold Coast. No one has written about this place, this time, this way.

    Judy Irving
    Filmmaker, *The Wild Parrots of Telegraph Hill*

Blending history, poetry, prose and photography, *River Town Girl* subverts and transcends, haunts and surprises. Part memoir, part ode, Litterine's stunning love letter to Edgewater, New Jersey, defies convention.

    Susan Coll
    Author, *The Stager*

RIVER TOWN GIRL

A MEMOIR

Lynn Litterine

River Town Girl: A Memoir

Copyright © 2020 by Lynn Litterine

All Rights Reserved

Published by Serving House Books

Copenhagen, Denmark, and South Orange, NJ

www.servinghousebooks.com

ISBN: 978-1-947175-28-0

Library of Congress Control Number: 2020937897

No part of this book may be used or reproduced in any manner whatsoever without the prior written permission of the copyright holder except for brief quotations in critical articles or reviews.

Member of The Independent Book Publishers Association

First Serving House Books Edition 2020

Cover Painting: Boat Landing Edgewater, N.J., by Godfrey Leeman, 1959

Author Photograph: Marc Kaufman

Serving House Books Logo: Barry Lereng Wilmont

To Marc Kaufman, my best partner on all adventures, and to the late Roger Beirne, who told me years ago that I'd write this book

PART ONE
UPSTREAM

Littoral

An edge in constant motion,
At the shoreline,
The infinitesimal gradations
Of ebb and flow.
The land, rock in all its forms,
Unmoving next to the restless water.
Planets tug.
Winds blow.
Salt water tips back
And forth in the great bowl.
Waves hit the land again and again.
Their sound moves across open air
And reaches a human ear.

My First Memory

I am standing on a stool and looking out a front window of our apartment. I must be about three because I need the stool to see out. On tiptoes, I can lift my eyes to just above both the sill and the bottom of the wood sash. Beyond them I see the Hudson River and a big boat headed toward a bridge.

Geology, Geography, and the Page I Write On

The Palisades that line the Hudson River are basalt cliffs that erupted near the end of the Triassic Period. About 200 million years ago, molten magma forced its way upward into sandstone then cooled and lay hidden inside the softer rock. Eons of rain, snow, ice, and wind wore away the sandstone, leaving columns of the harder rock. This rock is eroding, too, but much more slowly than the sandstone did.

The Palisades

Photo by Author

The cliffs rise from 300 to 540 feet above the river, parallel to its bank and so close to the water that only a sliver of land fits between the cliff face and the shore. For about three miles running along the river, starting just south of the George Washington Bridge, Edgewater, my hometown, occupies that sliver of land. The cliffs, the town, and the river form wavy parallel lines. On the far shore, Manhattan traces a fourth line.

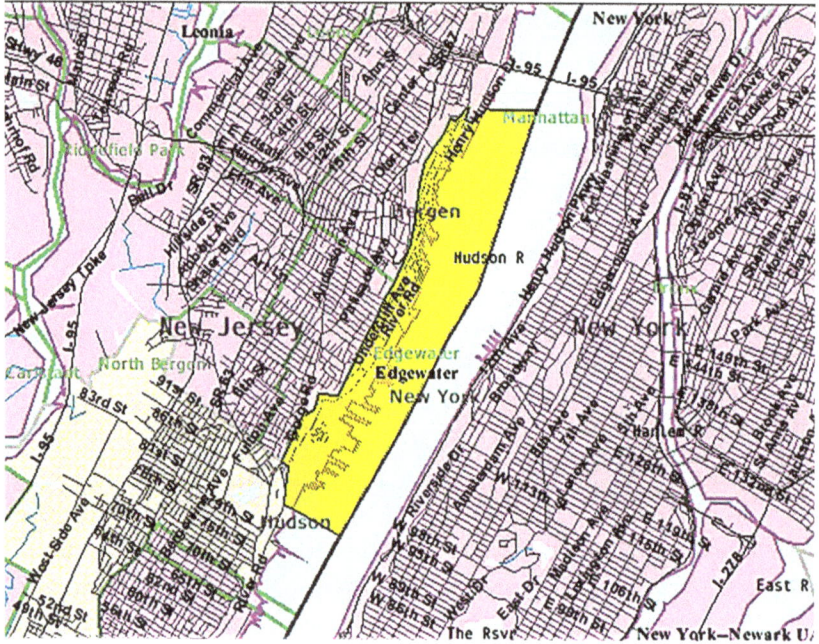

Edgewater is more river than land

U.S. Census

Now high-rise buildings along the river's edge and the cliffs encircle my once-blue-collar hometown. The buildings are dull slabs compared to the delicate tracery of the George Washington Bridge. Their flat uniformity is also unequal to the warm colors and weathered rock of the massive cliff face.

Buildings block the river view I grew up with, and their fences and gates enforce exclusive access to the shore I explored freely as a child. On the cliffs, high-rises loom so far above the town that the sun sets earlier than it did in the 1950s when I was young.

Photo by Author

Childhood and the town as it was exist now only in my memory. The text of its old day-to-day life is fading. But in my mind, I write, edit, rewrite, re-edit, and shape my stories, and I can be in that Edgewater again. I see the facts through an imagination cultivated in a solitary childhood among small-town eccentrics. It was a town that fed imagination, and I was an observer, a reader of books, and an ultimately justified believer in the power of stories.

... the shore I explored freely as a child

Author's Photo

My Imaginings from History

When I narrow my eyes as I look at the river, I can erase the buildings of Manhattan and the great span of the bridge. I can travel across time. I can envelop myself in the deep silence that surrounded the Lenni Lenape. Or smell the sweat of fear on the *Half Moon.* I can feel my toes freezing in a rocking rowboat while Revolutionary soldiers talk on and on about battle plans. Or I can sink back with a sigh into the soft leather seats of the town's first car. I embroider the facts left behind and enter other lives.

The Lenni Lenape
Time Immemorial

I am with everything here. Moving through the summer forest I shape the wind that blows around me. In the cold I bend to the wind's hard edge. In the river I shape the water flowing around me. In the cold I walk on its gray ice. I kill game and catch fish. I eat them and they become me. The catamount in the deep forest or the worms in the dirt will eat me and I will become them. Passing between the trees, passing among the animals, among my people, among my ancestors, I have always walked here.

N.C. Wyeth
The Outing Magazine,
Vol. 1, no. 3 June 1907

Henry Hudson
1609

19th Century Illustration/Wikipedia

The wide expanse of the river and the depth of the silence that surrounds us are what is real. Now the buzzing hive of Oost-Indisch Huis, so far to the east, is the dream. No coins clinking here to make fortunes for the fat Dutchmen who never leave Amsterdam. My ship and my worn, unhappy crew are what pass for the Company's power in front of this giants' palisade of stone. Eyes watch us from shore. Verrazano met them. They wore skins and hunted with spears and bows. Am I to explain to them the Company's chartered right to trade in this wilderness?

My men are frightened. No matter what the Company's charter claims may be, the men know we do not belong in this amplitude of beauty and mystery. Juet, in his fear, looks for reasons to shoot the natives as he did farther north. He is a man filled with mean tempers. The gulf between us and them is so wide that reasons will easily be found to kill them. Is that all that will come of this voyage? Have we traveled all this way to learn nothing new in the end?

When we have silenced their voices with death, their world will close forever. Juet, my frightened men, and the Company itself, *will* have them dead. Much the better for trade. New World colonies and Cathay spices are what the Company looks to, and only those riches will satisfy it. It has no interest in this wide river leading north, at first into shallows and then who knows how far or to what. It senses no riches there.

Burdette's Boy
November 15, 1776

It is so cold tonight, and I cannot stop shaking from it. And it is the cold that makes me shake, not fear. I am already 16, a man, and I can do a man's work. When William pointed to the biggest keg on the landing and challenged me to lift it, I did. Father calls me Spindle Shanks, but he asks me to come when he takes the ferry across the river in a storm.

When will they finish this battle parley so I can row home? The officers whisper on and on with General Washington. The wind has whipped up, and I want to take my hands off the oars and put them in my pockets. They feel like stones. It is so hard to hold the boat steady when I cannot feel my fingers. But I could not face Father if any harm came to the General. I just wish he would sit down while he talks so my boat can settle a bit. He is so big, and every time he shifts his weight the boat lurches, and he risks a tumble into the river.

On the Hudson (Burdette's Landing),
John George Brown (1831-1913), 1867

Fine Arts Museums of San Francisco.
Gift of Mr. and Mrs. John D. Rockefeller 3rd

It is easier to make these secret trips across the river alone. I will count us lucky this time if the Redcoats do not shoot from shore again. Three nights ago, they shot one of my oars in half. Only Providence kept that bullet from my head. Mother had sewn reports into my jacket lining for the officers at Fort Washington. I could not turn back. So I paddled the rowboat like a canoe the rest of the way across. My weight dug the bow down into the water. That made for slow going! But Father and the General had trusted me as they would one of the regulars. And for a week I had been rowing reports back and forth in the night. I knew the eastern shoreline well by the time I lost that oar. So, when I landed a mile too far south, I walked the boat back along shore until I drew near Fort Washington. An officer had come to meet me on the bank of the river.

"We thought you had gone missing, Peter," he said.

"Never, sir," I told him. "God willing."

"Good man," he said. "Now, Peter, let us have the papers and see what the General's thinking is."

But tonight, I rowed the General himself, and in two rocking rowboats mid-river, he plans with his officers from the east bank tomorrow's battle for Manhattan. I wish I could hear what they say. But their voices are low, and the wind blows noisily across my ears. Best to attend to the oars. Though this boat may be small, I am its captain, and they depend on me for the completion of their parley.

At least we are mid-river, only halfway back across to home. I can see our lights from here. If they finish planning soon, the tide will be starting to change, and the slackened current will make my haul back north to the Landing easier. The faster the better in this cold. I hope the fire is roaring and Mother has a bit of spirits for me too. And I hope she makes flapjacks again tonight.

George Washington
July 21, 1780

This is what comes of the brigadier general's unbounded imaginings—failure and humiliation. I told Wayne, "Think beyond that first moment of the encounter and conflict, think prudently, think all the way through to where the battle can be won." But he, predictably, skipped over the hard planning to be done in considering the possibility of failure. In neglecting that planning, he lost sight of whatever the tactic was that must have logically, necessarily been employed next to ensure victory. No wonder he is called "Mad" Anthony.

His thinking is never thorough, never set on strategy, and so he wound up harum-scarum chasing cattle on the west bank of the river. Three regiments and four cannon against 70 Royalists, the numbers were in his favor. But the Royalists' small arms pecked away, and Wayne lost control of his own men, who advanced for naught and then retreated. So, 18 of our men are dead, and 46 are injured. The blasted blockhouse still stands, and Bull's Ferry is lost. Even worse, it is lost in a way to make us appear foolish. And what are the rich returns on Wayne's glorious adventure? The scrawny cows his men caught and Major Andre's mocking poem to follow us through history.

Two Centuries at the Buena Vista 1780 to 1980

I speak as the presiding spirit here. I arrived when the main building was finished in 1780. A beautiful location overlooking the river—*buena vista* means "good view." The Hudson stretches a mile wide here, and the hotel looked out across that expanse. Guests could see a mile upriver and a mile down. With the bit of height from the hill, breezes came through even in summer. Most of the windows were put in the east and west walls to take advantage of that. Being so near the river ferries to New York, this small hotel prospered, enough for an addition in 1835. Leisure in the country was always the point. The teamsters and farmers taking goods and produce to New York never stayed here. It was fine sorts from the city looking to escape the heat and the stink of animals, smoke, and sewers. Some larger, fancier hotels were eventually built along the shore—my goodness, one even had a rollerskating rink. But this little jewel was a quiet haven. You could take a picnic out onto the grounds and watch sailboats and ferries crisscross the river all afternoon. And if you took a catnap while you were at it, who could blame you?

The building's been other things, too, over time. A shoe factory once, which is why its floors tilt toward the river. The heavy machines were on that side. A military academy at another time. But for more than 100 years, it was usually a hotel and usually oriented toward New York City. In fact, the owner in 1870 raised a large sign on the east side of the hotel that said "Sarah Bernhardt." Of course, that made little sense, but renaming it worked wonders for a while. Quite a few New Yorkers came across for a stay. Even the Divine Sarah herself came during the 1870s.

The American News Company/Author's Collection

And she was not the last of the show business types who came as guests. After the turn of the century, Fort Lee started turning out movies. The Palisades were the very cliffs where "cliffhanger endings" were filmed. Then you could run into Mack Sennett, John and Lionel Barrymore, even Mary Pickford, at the hotel. The world-famous magician Black Herman—and that is how he billed himself—once stayed here. I don't happen to know what his arrangements were. Life was strictly segregated then, but the hotel catered to an arty crowd, and perhaps that and his celebrity earned Black Herman some leeway. Now, Ruth St. Denis, she was Jersey born, but by the time she stayed over at the hotel, she was famous around the whole country. Her costumes and her dances were lovely, of course, but she burned enough incense in her room to choke the poor chambermaid.

Well, the glamorous times passed. Eventually the two buildings became a bar and apartments, both used just by the locals. The one thing that didn't change was the view. Now the windows frame the New York skyline and the George Washington Bridge. At night, when all those lights are on and winking back off the wide, dark river, it's still truly a *buena vista*.

Mary Parish, Victorious
19th Century

There are more taverns in that town than you can shake a stick at, but I took a stick to 'em all. Dark dens where a family's money turns into beer and goes down some man's gullet. Food for his children? No! Warm coats? No! Shoes? No! Just a river of beer down his throat. Oh, the tavern owners' children have food and coats and shoes all right. They're warm and well cared for, and I don't grudge 'em that. But the poor little runny-nose urchins in the rented flats don't see a fruit or a vegetable from one day to the next. Skinny little gray things they are. So I closed the taverns myself for a while.

I left home one night, walked down the hill, and went in the first tavern I came to. I had my walking stick that can hold off a bulldog if I need it to. I took it to the bottles along the wall. Caught those men by surprise, I did. Some little old lady comes into your tavern, you don't expect she'll take a stick to your liquor bottles. I broke their mirrors, too. And the gas lights. You shoulda seen them men run to shut off the valves! Then I left and I just kept going. The Lord was with me that night. All along River Road, one tavern after another, I shut 'em all. And not one of those fellas would press charges against me. Police dragging off an old lady is worse for business than cleaning up the mess I made. I cannot tell you the satisfaction it gave me.

Castles in the Air
1918

The river and the cliffs were perfect, enough like the Danube to soothe my wife's homesick heart. I made a lot of money in America, so I bought all the land from the hilltop down to the road into Edgewater. And I built a great white dream of a house up there on the hill. There were river views from almost every window. And that river is a beauty! I liked seeing the lights of New York as much as a mountainside in the old country.

Where I really had some good fun was with the hill itself. I built tunnels into the hillside like a real castle would have. Although my tunnels led to dead ends, from their entrances you could not tell that. They might have gone into the heart of the hill and had a secret staircase from each of them up into the house--one hidden behind a false panel in the music room, another coming up under the floor of the pantry, yet another next to the fireplace in my study. I ordered local bluestone for the tunnels' entry arches and walls. The height was such you had to walk into them bent slightly forward. That gave them a feeling of secrecy. Many Austrians and Northern Italians lived in Fort Lee then, and those men knew how to use a chisel on stone.

I really pleased myself—at some cost, too—with the red stone seats I placed near my tunnels. They were shaped like capitals for columns and carved all around with creatures, some like crested eagles and others with dragon's heads. I had them made back home and shipped to me. To ship solid stone is not an easy or cheap thing to do, but the local stone carvers could never have come up with the creatures I wanted. To carve those, you need men who have seen real castles. My capitals were two feet tall, just high enough for nice seats from which I could watch the river. As things went, I should have watched the town behind me more carefully and built myself some real tunnels!

I was content in my castle, but others in the world were not. It was the war in Europe that ruined our life on that beautiful hill. Our trouble started in April 1917, when President Wilson asked Congress to declare war against Germany. The Germans were courting Mexico on his southern border, and German submarines cruised in the North Atlantic. It took but four days for Congress to agree. And here we were, you see, me and my family, Germans in a big white house atop a hill on which I had created a little bit of our homeland.

... carved all around with creatures

Photo by Marc Kaufman

So, the townspeople stopped passing the time of day with us. Even the tradesmen, who were still happy to take our money, said little. Angry looks followed us on the street. We and our servants American citizens all, I must point out. We left the house less and less. In the first part of 1918, I found the word "KRAUTS" scrawled on our front wall. For certain, we were uncomfortable, but I thought we could ride out the war.

In those days I employed for small chores the young son of an Austrian family in town. He must have been but six or seven years old. He, too, felt the chill of having come from a country on the wrong side of the war. After the United States declared war on Austria-Hungary at the end of 1917, he told me that only one boy in his neighborhood was still allowed to play with him. And that child's parents had come from Germany. The little boys avoided everyone but their own families and each other.

It was early one afternoon in 1918 when the urchin arrived at my home clearly upset. He was reluctant to tell me why at first. Then, haltingly, his news came out. That morning, he'd taken a shortcut around the back of a tavern on Main Street but pulled up short when he saw some rough-looking men conferring there. Boys are as curious as monkeys, so he carefully slid closer along a wall to eavesdrop on them. The men, he told me, were planning to set fire to my house late that night. They had used cruel words that he would not repeat. I thanked him for the warning and gave him a dollar for his kindness. Then I told my driver to take him home and come back quickly. I set the whole staff and my wife to packing up everything of value, and we fled to a hotel in the city. If you can pay your bill, New Yorkers don't care where you or your parents were born.

We never moved back to my little castle. Over the day that followed our departure, my driver made enough trips to bring us what we wanted from what remained there. We stayed in New York until after the war, when we bought a house farther upriver on the east bank. It has no hilltop view to remind us of the Danube, but I find that I think less and less about the Old World. This Hudson River is enough in its own right.

The Arts in Edgewater Between 1910 and 1933

And there were many arts being produced: world-class tapestries, all manner of paintings and prints, engaging poems and manuscripts, films. New York was just across the river, and Edgewater beckoned as a pleasant, wooded place to work.

The lithograph below is by George Overbury "Pop" Hart. He was a successful painter and printmaker and, sometimes, an Edgewater resident. The print is called *Sunday Picnic on the Hudson*. A squirrel sits on a boulder and watches two men playing quoits. Another man has just come out of the river into the breeze and is shivering as he watches them too. A couple is kissing, and a bald man sleeps in a rowboat with his head on a big white pillow. A child in the foreground chews a straw and smiles at his dog. Could this be Double Docks? My father swam there as a kid. Surely Hart did, too. Maybe that is my father in the foreground with his dog, Bobby.

Harris Brisbane Dick Fund, 1923
Metropolitan Museum of Art

I recognize both the everydayness of this scene and the matter-of-fact approach that Hart, who painted houses and movie sets when he needed money, took to his fine art. He once answered a question about his painting this way:

> *The funny part of it is I didn't get started to make pictures to sell. I had my shack and a little money saved, and I thought I'd have a good time ... Making drawings is the best fun there is. Sure it's fine if the [sic] sell. Sort of surprises you though.*
>
> (Library of Congress, Manuscript Division, WPA Federal Writers' Project Collection, Edgewater Historical Survey, 1936, WPA Project #693)

You may be, as Hart was, a friend of Edward Hopper, and you may hang out, as Hart did, with Ashcan School artists in New York, but you still don't put on airs about your art in a working-class river town.

The First Car Owner, Mrs. Barnold

It's unusual for them to see an automobile on their streets, much less a lady driving it. And a lady of a certain age at that. Well, if he must travel then I must travel. That's only fair! When he takes the show on the road, I don't even have the animals to distract me at home. Such clever creatures they are. Of course, it's all his training. He has great patience with them. And with me, too. Surprising me with this beautiful automobile! "This will perk you up a bit while I'm gone," he said when he led me out to the side yard. And there it was. So shiny, I could see the trees and sky reflected in its fenders. Inside, it smelled wonderful, a *de luxe* smell from the leather bench seats, one in front and one in back. Why, six or seven people could sit in there. And it's a pleasure being up so high, even though I have to climb in from the running board and it's hard keeping my skirt decent and my hat on as I do.

I ground a few gears learning how to work the clutch, but it all feels quite natural now. Every day I take a spin in my automobile up and down River Road. I watch people's heads turn to look at me. Then I drive straight home and pull into the driveway. I don't stop anywhere along the way because I haven't learned how to park yet.

Glands
1930

I get so jumpy in school I hafta do somethin'. Maybe make a loud noise or get up and leave the room. They all laugh, 'cept the teacher, who looks like she wants to chew my head off raw. Even Doc Buckley, he's nice enough but he keeps sayin' I should get these gland shots. He keeps sayin' these shots will let me behave proper. Well, are they gonna change how stupid I feel? Yep, that's the problem. I'm stupid. My brain don't work fast, so how's my pee-too-a-terry gland gonna make me smart? That gland's not right, Doc Buckley says. He says I need six months of shots. Holy Hell! Six months of shots? He says I hafta stop duckin' school and hittin' kids and sassin' grownups, so I need them shots. But can them shots make kids not say mean things to me? Nope. Even if I get some shots, they'll keep on sayin' I'm bad and I'm stupid and I live on a crumby old houseboat and I smell. Then I get so mad. I rubbed a kid's face with poison ivy once. When that didn't shut 'em up, I brung a knife to school. But I wasn't gonna hurt nobody! Just shut 'em up! I'm known all over town for bein' bad. I even been in a New York newspaper. *Gland Cure Ordered for School's Bad Boy*—that's the headline. Says it right there. I'm the school's bad boy. Extry! Extry! Read all about it! Says them shots are gonna "make normal a 12-year-old boy" and that would be me. You can read about it in the newspaper.

27

A Flammable Town

In history ...

Kids often saw, heard, and smelled fire in Edgewater. It had an appetite for the town. And when the flames of factory fires hurt or killed workers, they made clear to kids how unpredictably combustible their working-class world was.

> *The Shadyside village was badly wrecked in 1901 by a series of explosions caused by a fire in the Barrett Co. Several plant buildings were blown apart and the majority of homes in the village were damaged by flying bricks and metal.* ("Village Badly Wrecked," New York Times, June 20, 1901.)

> *Later in 1901, fire heavily damaged the Bulls Ferry Chemical Co., covering three blocks.* ("By Fire-Chemical Works at Shady Side, N.J. Destroyed," Lima Times Democrat, October 16, 1901.)

> *Chemical operator Lorenzo Assele was working near a boiling kettle when it overflowed onto combustible material, starting the fire and subsequent explosions.* ("Chemical Works Burned," New York Times, October 17, 1901.)

> *Another devastating fire struck the Barrett Co. in 1903. The fire started in the building manufactur-*

ing tar paper. ("Whole Village Fought Fire," New York Times, September 16, 1903.)

A fatal explosion occurred at the Bulls Ferry Chemical Co. in 1904. Superintendent F. A. Hammer and chemist John Koelach were alone in a building when it was demolished by the explosion. Koelach, who was 34 years old and lived near the plant, was taken out dead with both arms missing. Hammer ... died while being taken by ambulance to the North Hudson Hospital. ("Fatal Shady Side Explosion," New York Times, November 2, 1904.)

An explosion in the New York Glucose Co. in 1906 injured 20 men. The roof of the building was blown off and the wreckage caught fire. ("Steam Explosion Badly Hurts Many," Fort Wayne Sentinel, May 22, 1906.)

A huge fire in 1907 ... began in the cellar underneath the engine room [of the Valvoline Oil Co.]. ... Firemen kept the blaze from spreading to ten large tanks filled with oil. ("$150,000 Loss By Spectacular Blaze," New York Times, August 2, 1907.)

Articles cited above are from http://www.colorantshistory.org/ShadysideChemInd.html

By 1912, the town was one of the few in the county with a paid fire department, and it needed one. Its volatile industrial mix by then included refined sugar, car parts, linseed oil, anthracite and bituminous coal, muriatic and sulfuric acid, dyes, coal tar, lubricating oils, airplane parts, and artillery shells—among other things. All this was being processed in 2.421 square miles sandwiched between the river and the cliffs. (*Industrial Directory of New Jersey*, 1918, p. 167)

A Flammable Town

On my street ...

Throughout my 1950s childhood, fire would still leap up unexpectedly and threaten the cheek-by-jowl wood houses of Edgewater. Cheap oil heat kept radiators hissing and dried the wood houses to fine kindling. Old electric wires twined among the dry wood planks. And many people smoked. At 12 or 13, kids smoked in hidden places like the woods or on abandoned docks. In those places, the glowing end of a cigarette tossed away as kids scattered could land on dry leaves, wood, or rubbish. That little fire could reach industrial buildings nearby. Kids and cigarettes—that's what I heard happened before the big Sugar House fire.

> *"Jack Frost Sugars" was the brand name of National Sugar ... The plant closed in 1942 due to the shortage of sugar in World War II. A fire destroyed most of the abandoned site in 1954.*
>
> http://www.colorantshistory.org/ShadysideChemInd.html

That last, matter-of-fact sentence doesn't capture the size and intensity of the 1954 blaze. By then, the Ford Motor Co. stored new cars in the building, and their gas tanks and rubber tires made a potential bomb of each one.

And the sentence doesn't capture the fright I felt on the day of the Sugar House fire. I was only eight and already a worrier, but older and tougher kids than me were scared that day. I was home with my mother after school, and we were intent on what we were doing. I was trying to turn a scrap of pale blue fabric into a doll's dress as the sunlight faded and we turned the lights on. The lowering darkness seemed to precede a storm. But when we went to the front window to take a look at what promised to be a huge storm, no wind blew and no whitecaps dotted the Hudson. Instead, clouds of black smoke billowed up from the waterfront a mile south of us. An orange glow lit the underside of the smoke. It was a fire and it was a big one.

We ran down three flights of stairs from our apartment to the street, where our neighbors were gathering. By the time we got there, the town's sirens were blaring. A fireman's wife who lived behind us arrived and said her husband had been called in from his day off. The old Sugar House was on fire, she said. "Doesn't Ford store cars there?" someone asked her. She gave a tight nod.

Along with the black smoke, sparks were floating north from the fire. They were falling on houses a mile or more from the blaze. Inevitably our rooftops began to smolder. People ran to get hoses to wet them down. But even if the water pressure had been normal--and it wasn't by this point--garden hoses had no chance of reaching the roofs of three-story houses built on a hill.

Sirens went off in Fort Lee and Cliffside Park, and soon their fire trucks were barreling down Fort Lee Road and Route 5, Oxen Hill and Gorge Road. Engines roared as they raced along River Road. Our fireman neighbor's son started to cry. He was a big kid, three years older than me, but soon was crying so hard that he threw up. "My dad's gonna die, my dad's gonna die," he chanted between sobs. I wanted to run from the fire and our smoldering roofs, but my mother stood still. I was scared she would wait too long to get away. I pulled on the corner of her apron. "I want to go," I said as quietly as I could manage. I didn't want to hear myself sounding frightened. "Don't be silly. We'll be fine," she said. If my strong, practical father had said it, I might have believed him. But my mother was a soother of fears, and she didn't like to see me upset. Against the chaos of the fire and against the fear I already sometimes felt for no reason, her words did nothing. Something wild and dangerous lay below the quiet surface of life. My mother stayed right there on the street with our neighbors. She wasn't going anywhere, so I clamped down hard on the fear I felt.

Eventually fireboats from New York pulled up near the Sugar House dock and pumped streams of river water onto the blaze. More fire companies arrived from all over the county, and our town, only three blocks deep between cliffs and river, was filled with them. Most were at the main fire, but others came to streets like ours and pumped water onto smoldering roofs. In the end, our houses were saved. The old Sugar House burned down, and the smell of its smoke lingered everywhere until the next big rain. I overheard some grownup say that kids had been hanging out on the Sugar House dock and smoking. Old wood, kids, and cigarettes— another kind of classic Edgewater fire.

A Flammable Town

In the night, in bed,
in my head ...

Edgewater was a small town. On any day of the week, I knew all the people I passed on the street. In such a small town, fires were intimate events. The spectators who showed up at fires, kids included, knew the name of each fireman and policeman rushing past. We knew the people who had escaped and were standing nearby with sooty faces and eyes clouded with shock. We knew the people who died in fires, too. Industrial roofs collapsed on firemen. Explosions blew workers apart. Old grandparents or children got trapped in back bedrooms.

One afternoon in the 1950s, sirens went off and fire trucks and police cars sped to the three old buildings on River Road known as The Flats, St. John's Flats in full, but no one ever said all that. Twinned four-story stacks of railroad flats joined by a central hall formed each building.

Some of us kids were gathered among the adults in front of The Flats by the time firemen carried out a stretcher. A little girl, a schoolmate, was on it. She was still alive; her face was uncovered. But that face, so familiar to us from school and church and playing in the streets, had changed beyond our understanding. The skin of her face was wrinkled and stained a light brown. She looked like an apple left too long on the sill. A newsman's camera flashed and lit the scene in white light. Parents turned us away and took us home, but it was too late.

The photo was on the front page of the next morning's newspaper, right next to the Rice Krispies and orange juice on the table. She had died, a child just like us.

In the weeks to come, I pretended to forget, but her wizened face was with me in school and in church and, most troubling, in bed at night. That was when I stared hard into the darkness and tried to know what her death was. But that vast fact was inconceivable. For a while, I was conscious of her face with me when I lay awake at night, but in time I left the conscious thought behind.

My Town in the 1950s

Edgewater

The town is alive.
Presses beat its heart's rhythm day and night,
Shaping aluminum, pushing it on.
Factories exhale breath of bitter linseed, banana oil,
And roasting coffee beans.
Along the one main road, the smell of stale beer
Drifts out tavern doors, a weary welcome smile
To the men coming off shift.
Buses and cars circulate like blood along that main road,
Carrying tired workers home, fresh workers to the factories.

The town speaks.
It whispers in small waves on the mud flats
When the tide changes from ebb to flow.
It chatters in tire chains
That pack down the sun-glinting snow.
It shrieks in sirens
To signal flames in a factory or an old railroad flat.
Every night at 8,
9 in the summer,
It blasts a curfew
To chase kids 16 and under off the streets.
No use claiming we didn't hear the horns

Bolted to telephone poles all over town,
Horns loud enough that, standing below them,
Our teeth ring with the blast.
After the curfew, silence takes over the streets.

The town tastes iron
From rusting chain-link fences,
From gears in the abandoned ferry house,
From broken machines left in factory yards,
From all the castaway scrap of industrial work.
It tastes the bitter coffee brewed in kitchen percolators
And in the hourglass carafes at the diner.
It tastes Miller High Life, Budweiser, and Rheingold.
It tastes penny candies and ice pops
In unnatural tones of pink and green and blue.
It tastes oily, rich shad netted in the river as winter turns
    to spring
And smoked in riverside sheds where their skin turns gold.

The town sees with a thousand window eyes.
They glow under apricot skies of rising suns.
They glitter when the moon hurls light off the river's surface.
And those same night eyes fling back across the water
The city's grid of winking lights.

The Human Tide

We children ... of different heights but always thin; skin that is pallid, rosy pink, or olive, but not all the colors of humanity, not yet; so many redheads, with and without freckles, that grownups joke "It's from the water."; Roman Catholics, who say A-MEN after the Lord's Prayer in school, Episcopalians and Presbyterians, who say AH-MEN, and a few Jewish kids who go to temple in other towns; in families with two siblings, with three siblings, with four siblings, with all the way up to 11 siblings, and, the rarest of birds, a few only children; Italian, Irish, English, German, Scottish, Dutch, Puerto Rican, Russian, and, after the revolution of 1956, Hungarian; boys in black Converse high-tops and girls in navy blue or white Keds, boys in Oxfords for church and girls in Mary Janes, and then, finally arrived at junior high school and adolescence, in saddle shoes and ballet flats and loafers and the boys still in black Converse high-tops; straight from school in our slacks or in our dresses or skirts and blouses then quickly into dungarees and corduroy pants and small-p polo shirts and cotton T's and back out onto the streets as fast as we can go, calling and yelling to each other ...

in constant motion ... skate wheels whirring and our keys on dirty strings around our necks to tighten the metal frames when they fall off our shoes halfway down a hill; vaulting fences and running across backyards; jumping rope with a clothesline and chanting "I am a pretty little Dutch girl, as pretty as pretty can be, be, be"; playing Flies Up with new "Spaldeen" balls that look and smell like Double Bubble gum; zooming down hills on bikes ("No hands!") to the slapping of playing cards stuck in the spokes of the wheels; bouncing balls and chanting "'A' My Name Is Alice and my husband's name is Al and we come from Alabama and with us we bring apples ..." swinging a leg high over the ball for every repeat of a letter all the way through the alphabet; eating nickel ice cream cones (a dime for two scoops), bright orange ice pops, big dill pickles, Baby Ruth bars, even pomegranates from the produce store when those are in season, 5x5 inch bags of Wise potato chips (some kids crush them into a fine meal in the bag first), Malty Balls, Buttons, and, from home, two Lorna Doones or Oreos (Hydrox for thrifty families) or Nutter Butters or even, halfway to candy, Mallomars, but just one then; smoking cigarettes stolen from our parents; boys playing baseball; girls watching boys playing baseball; whirling on the merry-go-round; pumping a swing so high its chains go slack then jumping off at that apex; playing Simon Says or How Many Steps Before the King? ("you may take one bath-tub step") or Hounds and Hares when one of us has chalk; sledding at the Public Service lot until our feet in red, black, or white rubber boots ache from the cold then go numb as stone so we have to limp home where we sit on big cast-iron radiators and finally get warm; skating at the ball field on the river where a flooded basketball court serves as our rink and town workers build a bonfire for us at night and playing Crack the Whip under the stars as Manhattan lies ignored across the river's dark expanse; always looking for each other, calling to each other, loudly making fun of each other ...

at ... The Ferry, a collective noun that includes a playground with a splash pool, an abandoned dock, a drugstore, a lunch counter eatery, a liquor store, above-store offices of doctors and insurance agents, and parking lots grouped where the 125th Street ferry used to come in from New York; the Ballfield, formally Veterans' Field, a square landfill jutting into the river just across River Road from the 10 little one-story houses joined in a row and known as The Vets' Housing; George Washington or Eleanor Van Gelder Schools where the grounds surrounding the two red-brick school buildings have playing fields and benches and swings and monkey bars and merry-go-rounds and see-saws; the foot of the cliffs where the woods provide dense cover and some big tree branches hold ropes to swing out over the hill that rapidly falls away to the backyards on Undercliff Avenue …

and on … the twisty streets of The Camps, where vacation tents and shanties of an earlier era have been replaced by snug little year-round houses; the two long north-south streets of the town and the short east-west streets that join them like the rungs of a ladder; the Pipeline, a tree-free swath of grass that covers the Transcontinental Gas Pipeline where it runs downhill from the cliffs under Palisades Amusement Park; the shore of the river where deserted barges and abandoned boats provide secret places to play, and treasures from the river wash up among the rocks or on the mud …

and

the adults … chubby women and skinny men or wiry little women and men with beer bellies and thin white legs; women in aprons on weekdays, in hats with half-veils on Sundays, or sometimes with handkerchiefs or just tissues bobby-pinned to the backs of their heads for a quick stop at confession; men in overalls, in chinos and well-pressed sports shirts, and, on Sunday, in suits and overcoats with their fedoras clipped to the backs of the pews in front of them; men and women in Chevy coupes and Ford Fairlanes (you are either a Ford family or a Chevy family), men in box trucks that carry their tools, in big pick-up trucks that collect the town's trash, in forklifts, bulldozers, and backhoes, and every vehicle, including the Fords and Chevys, has a standard transmission so "to drive" always means "to drive a stick shift"; men in the VFW, the American Legion, the Holy Name Society, and women in the PTA, the Order of the Eastern Star, the Ladies' Guild …

working ... in local factories on assembly lines or as foremen and on the borough trucks and cleaning the schools where only a few men teach and they come from out of town, delivering packages or milk or bread or mail, digging ditches, fixing plumbing or electric in the old houses, policing the town and putting out fires, typing, cooking school lunches (Little Red Hen--condensed tomato soup over toasted white bread—served on Fridays in deference to the Catholics who may not eat meat), in New York as steamfitters and sign painters and mid-level bankers; at home cooking and cleaning and sewing and watching the kids and sharing a cup of coffee and a cigarette with a neighbor on the front steps in the afternoon before starting supper ...

and sitting ... on the maroon plastic seats of bar stools; on bright red plastic seats of chrome-legged chairs in overheated kitchens; on the peeling and splintering wood of front stoops of what had once been one-family houses; on square honey-colored folding chairs at school for PTA meetings or at Borough Hall for council meetings; on dark wooden office chairs from the 1930s with seats planed to fit their buttocks and worn as smooth as satin; on big boxy easy chairs upholstered in cloth printed with green jungle leaves and coral-colored flowers; and all the while smoking Lucky Strikes or Sweet Caporals or Pall Malls or Raleighs, which come with coupons to collect and trade in for merchandise ...

and talking ... about work where they make aluminum pots or detergent or Hills Brothers coffee or any of the other things the town produces; about the price of marine fuel at Englewood Boat Basin or at the new marina in Edgewater ; about marriages, pregnancies, births, illnesses, and deaths; about the body someone found floating in the river; about the half-baked idea pitched by a guest speaker at the last PTA meeting; about the neighbor who put up new siding; about the teenager leaning toward trouble; about bar bets made in football pools or on whether 20 Mule Team Borax means a team of 20 mules or 20 teams of two mules each …

and on the river … on an early summer morning with the Sunday papers in a duffel bag on the floor of the boat and a paper sack of fresh jelly doughnuts to eat cruising north as church bells ring from First Presbyterian making clear what a stolen treat the river morning is; on a hurricane afternoon when the weather puts on a one-act play for everyone in town to watch except for the one man who alone and whooping sails his sloop over whitecaps like chalk marks on the river's surface; on a beery Saturday evening when a few men launch a plan to buy some shoreline and riparian rights for a boat club, friends then but not later, and no club is ever built; on the every-six-hours bustle at the shad fisherman's barge that signals changes in tides and the times to put the nets out then to bring the catch in then to put the nets out again then to bring the catch in again until the big, delicious fish have all gone upstream for the year…

Work, Love, Sweat

He's my father. He's a blue-collar man, and he loves his wife and child, so he works hard and takes care of them. That's why he works. That's how he loves us. He pays the rent. He pays for food. He pays electric bills and gas bills and doctor bills. He labors with his body, using it like any other tool in the box, and he sweats or he freezes as he works. In winter, his teeth are chattering by the time some leaking pipe is fixed. In summer, in a hot crawlspace, sweat drips from the end of his nose and runs down his chest. He swallows salt pills at lunch and changes his clothes. He sweats so much that everything--boxer shorts, chambray shirt, overalls, white work socks—gets thrown in the hamper at lunchtime and again before supper. On washdays the household cats roll in sweaty nests of blue denim and chambray on the floor near the washing machine. His smell affects them like catnip. Napping later they will still smell like his dried sweat.

Every penny he earns comes out of the sweat and muscle and blood of his body. One day his overalls get caught in a spinning gear at a factory, and he's bruised all over when they finally rip and he's thrown free of the machine. Good thing the denim was old and ripped easily. On another day he loses his grip on a cast-iron radiator he's carrying up some stairs, and, as it smashes his hand against the floor, it cuts the tips off two fingers. After that, his nails grow like a bird's claws out of the end of each chopped finger. He calls the two fingers "The Clutch," and I run screaming and laughing when he threatens to tickle me with them. On a different day, a screwdriver slips and bores into his forearm. OK, part of the job, but then the penicillin pills he takes for the dirty puncture wound lead to what the doctor calls "penicillin poisoning." Every day for a week a different part of his body swells. To control the swelling and keep him out of the hospital, my mother wraps him in sheets soaked in ice water. The cold feels worse than the screwdriver ever did because he's skinny, not a bit of insulating fat on him. His lips turn blue. He says nothing, just groans in the cold, wet sheets. A week passes before the swelling stops. He's never missed that many days of work.

Even normal wear and tear sculpts him. The calluses on his palms are so thick from twisting the handles of tools that he can't close a fist. His knees are covered in callus, too, but they can still bend. He can still kneel to work, but he no longer kneels for anything else. Instead, he gives work everything he's got and hopes that's understood in any world to come. And when the sweat and the pain and, yes, the boredom get to be too much, he has a cold beer at a local bar and maybe a second and a third and doesn't get home until it's late and he's sick to his stomach and anger's in the air.

How To Set Sail?

Stories begin in a gap between what is and what we think and feel and wish about what is. We sift raw facts through a consciousness grounded in time and force a beginning, middle, and end on them. This story begins in a silent, empty space between my mother and father. He's late for supper. It's 10:30 when he finally comes home from work, and he's been at a bar. Sometimes this chasm opens in him without warning. When it does, he drinks too much. At those times, he's not loud or angry but quiet and withdrawn. My mother meanwhile is both angry with him and afraid of the anger she feels. How much is she allowed to ask for? He comes home. The bills are paid. He injures no one except himself. She's afraid that her anger, if loosed, will lead to something worse. He was a wanderer before they met. Would he leave if she pressed hard against the drinking? She hates conflict and abandonment is her greatest fear.

She's relieved when he backs his truck safely down the steep driveway next to our house. He turns off the ignition and comes in through the basement door. He sits down there in his overalls in the dark for a while before he changes his clothes and slowly climbs the stairs. He walks past the dried-out chops, fried potatoes, and wilted salad still on the kitchen table and, instead, goes straight to their bedroom. He undresses and slips under the covers, saying nothing. My mother sits upright and silent on the living room couch. These are my parents at their hardest moments.

The silence that separates them at those times swells and fills our house. I'm their only child, and I am suspended alone in the space between them. Sometimes, like a solid thing, the silence presses against my chest until I feel I can't drag air into me. Sometimes I fear I will erupt, and the fear tightens my throat. I carefully inhale, slowly and deeply, relaxing the knot in my throat and drawing air down into my chest. I *can* still breathe. My parents are my world, and, in their angry silence, my world loses all certainty. Its color and warmth drain away. The possibility of this bleak landscape lurks in every afternoon. Our household does not relax until my father is home for our normal suppertime.

Photo by Marc Kaufman

My refuge from the bleakness is hardly original. Like many lonely children, I shed reality in the worlds of books. Back then, the blue, green, and red covers of The Companion Library books are fresh and new; 60 years later, their bindings taped and barely holding each book together, the remaining two will still sit on my shelf, *Hans Brinker or The Silver Skates*, about a poor Dutch boy whose father's brain damage has left him with vacant eyes, and *Treasure Island*, the best of all my books, in which Jim Hawkins sails off to scary adventures with a very complicated group of grownups.

On my parents' silent nights, I pick up *Treasure Island*. What can I make of Long John Silver, the peg-legged pirate who plots bloody mutiny but later saves Jim Hawkins's life? As I sink into the story, the night sky above the *Hispaniola* opens vast and inky blue. The wind smells of the salt ocean it blows across. Ropes and planks creak as the ship races through sea spray towards murder and gold.

I long to be Jim Hawkins, who dares to set sail. I need my father's strength and help to do that. He knows how. He rode freight trains through his high school summers. "A man of many adventures," it says under his senior yearbook photo. In the Class of 1928 Will, he bequeaths his "love for the road" to a friend of the teacher who wants company on her hikes. In the 1930s, he went to sea on cargo ships. I read in his journals about ports like Durban and Mombasa. But I can't trust him to help me. He falls into chasms without warning. I don't know why.

Treasure Island

BY ROBERT LOUIS STEVENSON

Illustrated by HENRY C. PITZ

Grosset & Dunlap, Publishers

NEW YORK

Treasure Island by Robert Louis Stevenson, Illustration by Henry C. Pitz, Grosset & Dunlap, 1947

The Adventures of Lynn and Claire

I meet my best friend Claire on the first morning of kindergarten. It's 1951. Claire is nibbling on a dog biscuit at the bus stop and offers me a taste of the Milk Bone, Large Dog Size. I don't have a dog and have certainly never tasted a dog biscuit. A new life is opening that morning, and I do not feel hopeful. When the school bus—which I have never before ridden on, this being kindergarten—comes, I will have to let go of my mother's hand and walk away until I am out of her sight and far from the cozy apartment that is our home. I hate leaving my mother.

Eleanor Van Gelder School
Photo by Author

This offer of a bite of dog biscuit is, I know, just the first unwelcome challenge of the long morning ahead. But I like Claire's friendly face, the red bows on her braids, and her apparent indifference to this change in our lives, so I take a piece of biscuit from her hand and nibble on it. It's gritty and dry and has almost no flavor. But I swallow it because Claire is smiling at me. When years have passed, all I will remember of that first school day is Claire and the taste of dog biscuit, how the corner across from the library looked while we waited for the school bus, and how scared I was to leave my mother. Claire and I may have held hands as we got on the bus. We may have sat together on the bus's hard brown seats or in the little enameled chairs in the kindergarten room. Certainly, we rode the bus home together after our first half-day at school.

On some later day, I'm allowed to go alone to Claire's house to play. The house is down a dirt alley and around the corner from mine. I can almost see it when I climb out my bedroom window onto the porch roof, but walking by myself, it feels like quite a journey. "House" isn't the right word for what either of us lives in, but "apartment" isn't the right word either. The houses in our part of town were built as one-family homes and later cut up into apartments. Only two apartments in my house, one of which my family rents. But Claire's house is big and has three apartments Her parents own the house and leave the top-floor apartment empty, a luxury, but it's right above their heads. I meet Claire's dog, Red Mike. He's a purebred Doberman whose shiny coat is the color of a semi-sweet Hershey bar. Mike is huge, but also like a Hershey bar, he's sweet. Maybe because Claire shares with him everything she eats except her chewing gum. He expects the best from her—and later, from me, too. We are his girls. Even the toughest kids in the neighborhood, the O'Sullivan twins, make way when we walk Mike down the street.

Claire and I share almost every day of childhood. We can spend an afternoon indoors playing with Ginny dolls, but we're happiest outdoors roaming the town. We're skinny little girls with scabbed, knobbly knees who like to run fast and make noise. We roller skate down Claire's steep hill. We throw snowballs at big kids then run away shrieking. We sneak back and forth through Miss Farr's yard. When she catches us, she never comes out. Instead, from behind the curtains on a back window, a voice orders: "Go right back where you came from." The voice runs chills up our spines and sends us scurrying. And it shames us a little, as if where we came from lacks something.

Inevitably, as we get bigger, we prowl the shore of the Hudson and climb over big boulders to get to the very edge of the river. We know we shouldn't be there on our own, but our mothers never find out. At high tide, we jump from rock to rock. At low tide, we hunt for burnt-out light bulbs washed up on the mud or caught among the now-exposed boulders. We throw the first bulb we find at a rock just to break the glass. But the result is better than expected. Pop! A tiny explosion. After that, we fire off every light bulb we find as we ramble along the shore. Light bulb after light bulb … pop! pop! … through years of childhood … pop! Some things in our lives will never disappoint us.

As We Roam the Town ...

The Things We See

Sun sequins sparkling on river water
Bone-white storm waves running against the gray tide
City windows reflecting sunsets
Headlights tracing the roadbed of the great bridge
Buildings like giants watching the river pass

The Things We Taste

Cherry-flavored jelly dollars
Sweet white meat of crab claws
Chinese love apple seeds
Salami and provolone sandwiches
Nehi grape soda and Black Jack gum

The Things We Touch

Silky, worn dock planks against bare feet
Tickly tiny legs of baby crabs on palms
Soft river mud squshing up between toes
Thick, stiff scabs on scraped knees
Itchy fuzz of plane tree seeds stuffed down clothes in ambush

The Things We Hear

>   Whisper of tiny waves when the tide changes
>   Whine of an ambulance on the West Side Highway
>   Growl of trucks up- and down-shifting on River Road
>   Screeching of raccoons in the woods
>   The grownups softly talking in the living room

The Things We Smell

>   Shad smoke on the early spring air
>   Gas fumes at the Texaco station
>   Stale beer outside the bars
>   Mommy's *Tigress* perfume by Faberge
>   Or Daddy's *Old Spice*

Our Princess Rode Bareback

A little girl dreams when told that her small town once had a real Indian princess who rode down its main street on a white horse. Suddenly the world's possibilities seem infinite. I saw that uninspiring ride in my childhood: middle-class homes with postage stamp yards; then working-class houses broken up into apartments; and, last of all, dingy clapboard buildings squeezed among factories in what was called with no irony "Shadyside." The town embraced those ugly factories. At its north and south ends on River Road, the same road once traveled by an Indian princess on a white horse, signs announced: *Edgewater: Where Homes and Industry Blend.*

The industrial part of town began in earnest with Alcoa Aluminum—a massive building painted in a shiny aluminum color. Our princess was buried in a tiny cemetery surrounded by the Alcoa factory because the factory, built in 1916, was the newcomer. In 1663, the queen of the Netherlands made the original land grant for the cemetery to the Vreeland family, and the blurred headstones on the oldest graves are Vreelands'. Later stones mark Revolutionary and Civil War veterans and two "devoted slaves," Isabella and Toby. In the 1950s, when I learned about our princess, people were still being buried there while Alcoa's presses boomed around them. This mixture of princess, queen, slaves, soldiers, and aluminum pots and pans and cookie sheets shaped odd imaginings. Strange characters had walked—and ridden—the workaday streets of Edgewater.

Every Brownie Scout in the town knew that Princess Gowon-go Mohawk was buried in the cemetery that lay between the arms of the U-shaped Alcoa factory. In our brown uniforms and felt beanies, we visited her grave with our troop leaders. Our own Indian princess! We little girls who watched TV—*Roy Rogers, The Cisco Kid, The Lone Ranger*—stretched out on the living room floor could daydream of adventure like the boys did. I imagined her long black braids, the silver and turquoise medallions on her white buckskin tunic, and her flourish of the reins as she turned her horse's big white head and galloped off, bareback of course! Dreaming on my back among the dandelions and pigweed in our back yard, I could almost feel the rush of wind across my face. She stayed in my imagination.

So, more than a half-century later, I trawled the Internet to see if I could find the princess again. She was there! The first hit was an essay by Mary Mapes Dodge in *St. Nicholas: A Monthly Magazine for Boys and Girls* (1873-1943). The essay, "For Boys and Girls Who Love Horses," is about two paintings by Gilman Low. One of those paintings is of Go-won-go Mohawk riding "her favorite horse Buckskin." Dodge describes the subject of the painting:

> ... [She] has given performances before the crowned heads of Europe ... [She is a] full-blooded Mohawk ... [and] never rides with a saddle ... [She was] obliged to make her horse rear at least a hundred times [for the painting] ... [She] made nearly all of her own and Buckskin's trappings [for the painting] ... [M]ore than 30,000 beads were sewn by hand on her suit ... so arranged as to form ornaments emblematical of her tribe.
>
> (St. Nicholas: A Monthly Magazine for Boys and Girls, November 1908, p. 55)

Even in the black and white reproduction of the painting, Go-won-go Mohawk's smile shines. She wears a headband with one long feather sticking up from the back. Animal tails that look like ermine hang from her beaded shirt, and her legs are wrapped to the knees in heavily fringed buckskin. This princess was familiar to me. Except for her bobbed haircut, she was my childhood dream of the Wild West.

Other online entries told me more. Born to a chief and medicine man in 1860, Go-won-go ("I fear no one" or, perhaps, "first flower") was taught to ride, to rope, and to shoot guns and bows and arrows. Only one job market existed for a woman with those skills, so the princess joined traveling Wild West shows. She appeared with Buffalo Bill Cody in *Buffalo Bill's Wild West*, where, according to published reports at the time, her role required her to ride two horses at once while standing on their backs. The reports add that she had "a splendid physique."

I found out that this princess was not demure. She was competitive and noisy. When she rode in races, she let loose war whoops to spook the other horses. Sometimes, she even whooped instead of knocking on doors when she arrived at someone's house for a visit.

Newspaper writers of the time described a compelling woman:

> *[H]er personality is so striking that when on the stage she dominates every-thing and everybody else.*

and

> *[She plays a] male hero, and her acting is so realistic at times that her sex is often doubted. ... Her physical strength is remarkable. She is able to throw the ordinary man clean over her head with the greatest possible ease.*

She performed that feat in *The Indian Mail Carrier (Wepton-no-mah)*, which she wrote, produced, and starred in. She made a tremendous hit with that play and with *Flaming Arrow* on two tours of England (1893-1897 and 1903-1906). A command performance was given for the future King George V.

Used by permission of the British Museum

A long silence follows those contemporary reviews before she reappears online. Now she is the focus of literary criticism. A 21st century audience, invested in the "outsider," appreciates her refusal to fit neatly into categories. In *The Indian Mail Carrier*, she played a male hero, a Native American who robustly avenges his father's death and enjoys a flirtation with a young white woman.

Christine Bold, a professor at the University of Guelph and writer on U.S. popular culture, has this to say in an online blog entry for the British Association of American Studies:

> *At some point in the 1880s, Go-won-go Mohawk seems to have broken the constraints of US wild west employment to build her own theatre troupe, including her non-Native husband Charles W. Charles. She wrote melodramas for her company to perform, creating for herself a fascinating gender-bending—perhaps Two-Spirited—identity on- and off-stage.*

Bold describes a self-assured woman of the theater:

> *... From her first interview, ... [s]he insisted on her difference from "[Buffalo] Bill's Indians," ... and she emphasized her agency as "actress-authoress." And she developed the variety act embedded in her melodrama into a cross-race, cross-empire virtuoso display, cleverly straddling multiple audiences and houses at a time of fierce debates about variety undercutting theatre. ... The cultural space which Go-won-go Mohawk enabled—a queer Indigenous transatlantic space of performance ...*
>
> http://www.baas.ac.uk/usso/eccles-centre-summer-scholars-series-vaudeville-indians-on-the-british-stage/

Well! A boundary-breaking, opinionated, gender-bender

sort of a princess! I was a long way from my Brownie troop's cemetery visit. My long-dead princess had taken her place in the world of modern ideas.

Then it was just a small step to "Gowongo Mohawk's Free West" and "The Gowongo Effect," sections in *Pioneer Performances*, a book by Matthew Rebhorn (Oxford University Press, 2012). Annie Oakley pales when the author, an associate professor at James Madison University, contrasts her with my princess.

> ... [Oakley's] entrance was always a "pretty one." "She never walked," Dexter Fellows, longtime press agent for the Wild West, noted. "She tripped in, bowing, waving, and wafting kisses" ... (7)

Then, citing the manuscript of *Wep-ton-no-mah*, Rebhorn writes,

> *Gowongo Mohawk ... did not enter wafting kisses or bowing but made her entrance with "fearless riding," which, it is crucial to note, she executed "without saddle or bridle." (8)*

Oakley, he adds, always rode sidesaddle.

He places Go-won-go Mohawk in a long line of performers who "interrupted, interrogated, and derailed the stories ... [Cody] told" (5).

Even better! An interrupting, interrogating, derailing sort of a princess. Someone who could outride Annie Oakley and, at the same time, place ironic distance between herself and the Wild West myth: She sometimes signed her photographs "Aboriginally yours."

Go-won-go Mohawk toured until her health failed. She died in Edgewater in 1924 after a stroke and was buried in the old cemetery where I first met her. The last entry I found about her online is a fit epitaph; alas, it's not on her headstone. A performance artist and blogger, Sabina England, writes:

> *I'd like for more people to know about her. She sounded like a total badass and I wish I could find copies of her plays.*
>
> www.SabinaEngland.com

A total badass kind of bareback-riding war-whooping princess from a factory town on the Hudson River. A tomboy princess. More than a daydreaming Brownie Scout could have hoped for ... she makes me want to yell a war whoop.

Used by permission of the British Museum

More Childhood Visions ...

An Indian princess is treasure enough for any small-town girl, much less one in a tiny working-class borough in industrial North Jersey. But an equally fantastical sight sometimes visited Edgewater when I was a child. In the 1950s, a Chinese junk used to show up now and then and dock in town for a few days.

Public Domain, https://commons.wikimedia.org/w/index.php?curid=332790

My father took me to see the junk whenever it docked. It was huge, but I was five or six years old and considerably smaller then, so maybe I misremember its size. It had a hull with a raised platform on each end and looked as if it came straight out of the pages of a storybook. I think the hull was black with dark orange trim, but it may have been brown and trimmed with maroon. The glossy paint made the junk shine like an enameled Chinese box. Its square sails were the color of parchment. I wish I could say more. I wish I could tell you where it came from or how often or why. But I lived in the present and accepted it at face value, no questions asked. A Chinese junk just shows up in town sometimes. The child I was did not even notice who was onboard the boat. I just stood on the dock, my hand in my father's hand, and took in the sight. The wider world seemed a wonderfully unpredictable place to have sent a Chinese junk to my town and to me. I accepted the vision and dreamt ever more deeply. There is lasting strength in that kind of dreaming.

Interpreting Life's Lessons

Edgewater was a small town, only 4,000 people, when I was growing up. But from those 4,000 people, eccentric characters and rich story lines spilled out of houses and onto the streets. Most people in town accepted these happenings as a matter of course. What they might mean caused little curiosity. People just did things. But this approach was not enough for my mother, a born storyteller. She'd identify a beginning, a middle, and an end in the apparent chaos. Then she'd gaze into the story she'd organized and draw instruction from it. As she cooked and ironed and sewed, or as she relaxed with a Kent cigarette and a cup of coffee, she'd share the lessons with me.

Benny Scott

A barge is a big, floating space, inelegant but well designed to carry bulky cargo, a boat, yes, but a boat with no get-up-and-go. Push it. Pull it. Initiative, in the form of engines, belongs to the red or green tugboats that move the barge upriver or down. If its cargo needs protection from the elements—grain, for example—the barge will have a wooden structure covering its top deck. If the cargo needs no protection, something like trap rock, say, just a sturdy wall at each end of the deck will hold the cargo in place. Both open and closed decks include tiny quarters at one end for the bargeman and, in summer, his family.

Many barges, open and closed, were retired to the mucky shore of the river along Edgewater. Some held homely little boat clubs. The clubs owned open barges to dry-dock boats in winter and enclosed barges where members could hang out and socialize. Around an old Pepsi machine, a refrigerator for beer, a stove to boil blue-claw crabs caught from the club dock, and a bumper-pool table at 25 cents a game, a year-round community formed.

But some barges were about solitude. The tiny living quarters became rough studio apartments for more-reclusive folks. The close neighbors—river rats, crabs, raccoons, and fish—were not nosy. And because the barges had been abandoned, the price was right.

When I was a child, this arrangement suited a man named Benny Scott. He was old, alone, and didn't have much cash, though I doubt that he thought of himself as poor.

Family Photo

With an informal electric line run from on shore by a handy friend and a few jugs of clean water for coffee (bathing did not loom large), he was snug. What little money he had he spent at the A&P in town. Canned beans and spaghetti, packaged crackers, and Mallomars. He loved Mallomars.

The public health nurse in town checked in every couple of months and told him to eat vegetables and fruit, but Benny was not interested. They didn't fill him up the way the carbohydrates did. The nurse, a local gal, knew he had diabetes, but Benny was a stubborn man and ate what suited him. She didn't bother leaving nutrition pamphlets from the county. But when things got to the point that she had to talk to Benny through his front door, she knew he was hiding something. She tried to peer into the two tiny windows, but he'd shut the curtains. Then she checked with Otto at the A&P. Had Benny been in for food? Not himself, Otto said, but every week a kid from town came to pick up a few things for him. Benny paid the kid to shop for the usual canned food and Mallomars.

The nurse knew her town and its residents well. They were private and proud and did not reveal hardship or like being told what to do. She was a master of diplomatic, oblique intervention, but, if she thought someone was in danger, she would force the issue. And, finally, she thought Benny was in danger. So she dispatched two cops, both of whom he knew. But Benny got his back up, so they had to kick down the door. He was in bed. A bad smell filled the room, and it came from Benny. When the bed sheet was pulled back, the big men saw ulcers on his feet and could tell that the ulcers were advanced.

So they called for an ambulance and carried him out to it—sputtering protests—as gently as they could. The ambulance attendant cut away Benny's pajama legs and saw more ulcers and, there is no way of saying this in good taste, the worms. They were maggots, and they were flourishing. First the ambulance stopped at the firehouse, where the men slowly and carefully rinsed off Benny's legs in the parking lot. Once he was marginally clean, they took him to the hospital. After treating the old man, a doctor said the maggots had kept Benny alive by eating the diseased tissue. This off-putting symbiosis had saved him from toxins created in his decaying flesh. A few weeks later, Benny was back home on his barge, healed and, temporarily, squeaky-clean.

My mother told me this story and interpreted its significance this way:

Even maggots can do some good.

Daisy Lee

Daisy Lee was a tiny, inconspicuous woman. She usually wore a brown overcoat and a knit turban, also brown, out of which stuck a few similarly colored wisps of hair. The overall effect was that of a field mouse. She lived in a house on our short, dead-end street with her brother. At late middle age, these siblings seemed left behind by a tide that had ebbed when their parents died. No one visited the house; no deliveries arrived at the door. Miss Lee kept house for her brother, and they both kept to themselves. He went to work; she ran the rare errand. And, ever mouse-like, her eyes would glitter with alarm if anyone spoke to her at the post office or the A&P. From outside their house, the blinking gray light from a TV was all that could be seen to move.

For years, nothing urgent forced this whispery presence beyond the outline of her small life. Then, only once, she came to my mother's door. To understand why this might have happened, picture my mother: a big, comfortable woman quick to smile. Perhaps Miss Lee intuited the rest; my mother had a compassionate heart, and her practical hands did its bidding.

When the doorbell rang that afternoon, I stayed upstairs while my mother went down to answer it. I could hear voices speaking low, and then the door clicked shut. I looked out the window and saw Miss Lee going back down the three flights of outside stairs. My mother's footsteps were slow as she climbed back up to our apartment. "How sad," I heard her say to herself before she came into the living room. I tried to read her face—I was expert at that--and while I saw sadness, I saw another feeling, too, the kind of look she wore when I disappointed her. She noticed me watching. "What did she want?" I asked. "Nothing, hon; it was nothing." What business could this phantom have had with my mother? I wanted to know. So I pestered and eventually wore my mother down.

"She asked me to help her with an enema," my mother said. The level of intimacy shocked me as it had shocked my mother. Miss Lee's familiar face belonged to someone who was nevertheless a complete stranger to us. It was as if a passerby had stopped my mother with the request, and it was beyond what even my big-hearted mother could do. "What did you say?" I asked. "I said no," she answered and sounded disappointed.

After that encounter, things went on as they always had among the neighbors on my street. Some years later, Daisy Lee died at home. Her brother must have found her that evening, must have called the doctor, and must surely have been told by him how she died. The neighbors simply saw a hearse come and carry her away.

Her brother then spent the next twelve hours cleaning out the house in time for morning garbage pickup. When the sun came up, a wall of white cardboard boxes covered the sidewalk that ran along their front yard. The stack was almost four feet high and eight feet long. The boxes were unopened; their cellophane wrapping reflected the morning sun. No one on the block would have considered picking over them, but the neighbors were curious. Finally, one took her dog for a strategic walk, and telephones began to ring. Every box, she reported, held store-fresh baby clothes. The box labels announced sleepers, sweaters, booties, undershirts, and diapers enough to take a newborn into toddlerhood. In this working-class town, where most houses were stuffed with four, five, six, and more children, Miss Lee had prepared carefully for the fulfillment of her dreams.

What my mother read out of this could have served as Daisy Lee's epitaph:

Every human heart yearns deeply.

Tom Lee

On that small dead-end street of my childhood, Tom Lee, Daisy's brother, kept a vivid secret of his own, although I was years past childhood when I learned it. In 1972 I was reading a book about tattoos that a friend bought for me because I'd recently gotten one. He bought it at the Columbia University bookstore, and it read like somebody's doctoral thesis. It took its topic very seriously. The book covered tattoos from early soot-and-needle-pricks through Janis Joplin's bracelets.

One of its stories was about a New Jersey man whose back carried a legendary tattoo. This multi-colored, gloriously detailed scene was of the Last Supper and had been inked by a tattoo artist in Greenwich Village in the 1930s. The picture took months to finish, according to my book, and the pain from all those needle stings must have been considerable. Nevertheless, the New Jersey man had shown up at the tattoo parlor across the river dozens of times before the work was finally done.

Funny, I told my father, the man had the same name—Tom Lee—as one of our old neighbors. "He's the same man," my dad said. "Don't you remember Tom Lee? Even in August, he wore a shirt. Didn't matter how hot it was, he stayed covered up." I hadn't noticed, which surprised my dad, who had faith in my perceptiveness.

My tattoo was a tiny one on my left hand. I enjoyed the transgressive pop it gave me, but my small rebellion was nothing compared to Tom Lee's. What had possessed our old neighbor to perform that extravagant act? I remembered a silent man living a colorless life. I didn't remember ever seeing him in church. I would never have suspected that he had turned his own back into an altarpiece. I could see there were implications to this. During all those years of childhood, while I came and went along my short block, preoccupied by the issues of a child's life, had there been a secret behind each and every door? Had I lived unknowing among a whole library of stories?

My mother made no pronouncement on this story, but I will:

A work shirt can hide a world of surprises.

Or, perhaps:

Big impulses bring big regrets.

Madame Florence

When the town's two elementary schools were changed to an elementary school at George Washington and a junior high school at Eleanor Van Gelder, I was starting fourth grade. My bus stop was switched to the intersection of Route 5, Undercliff Avenue, and Hudson Terrace. I passed Claire's house on the way and walked to and from the bus stop with her most days.

Where we waited along the east side of Route 5, four small houses stood. They were shingled in brown wood and had roofs that were reddish. The Rodriguezes lived in one with their two sons; Joe was in my grade. The Hoffmeiers lived in another with their three children. A third held a tiny grocery store run by Mrs. B. The Benedicts lived on the floor below the store.

The fourth house was a source of endless speculation by the children who waited for the bus. A small sign out front said "Madame Florence, Psychometrist." Look up that word today and you'll be referred to "psychometrician," a medical practitioner trained to create, standardize, administer, and interpret objective psychological tests. That was not Madame Florence's job. Madame Florence "read" objects.

Was your husband cheating on you? Bring his slipper or lighter to a session and let her hold it so it could "speak" the truth to her. Or bring your own scarf or glove for a free-form reading, and you might learn something you didn't know about your own life.

We children knew her only by sight, a short, round woman with sparse hennaed hair. She might leave the house or come home when we were nearby but not often. She never spoke to us. We were careful not to annoy her because, unlike the other adults in town, she had mysterious powers to focus on us.

The only entry reliably about her I could find online is an Oct. 22, 1942 clipping from *The Record* in Hackensack. It announces plans for two weeks of events in the St. Cecelia's Victory Fair. Mrs. William Conklin of Meadowbrook Road planned to host one of the events at her home, and "Madame Florence, Edgewater psychic, will tell fortunes."

Psychic. Fortuneteller. Accurate enough, but Madame Florence's sign read "Psychometrist," which had a much sturdier sound to it, and my mother stuck to that word. "She's the only person who can list herself that way in the phone book," my mother told me. (Apparently AT&T had high standards for legitimacy.) "Police departments have called her in on unsolved murders. I think one was in Texas."

My mother had her own reason for not writing off Madame Florence. When she was a very young woman living with her father and stepmother, she and some girlfriends went on a lark to a reading by Madame Florence. My mother handed over her handkerchief. After communing with the hanky for a few moments, Madame Florence told my mother to check the top drawer of her bureau because someone had been snooping in the letters she kept there. Mom checked when she got home and found the letters were mussed up. She blamed her stepmother, whom she'd never liked anyway.

My mother was no mystic, but she advocated an open mind:

There are more things in this world than meet the eye.

Henry Gaul

Henry "Henny" Gaul was a kind, courteous man who wore a brown corduroy coat in the cold and a neatly pressed, short-sleeved shirt when it was warm. His much-loved wife had died. He had no children. His job as chief clerk at the Valvoline Oil Company had ended in respectable retirement. So, in his 70s, he spent most days at the Undercliff Motor Boat Club, where, although now boatless, he was a longtime member and secretary-for-life.

Henry Gaul
Author's Photo

My parents belonged to the club, and, because it was only three blocks from our apartment, I spent a lot of time there. My friend Claire and I used to play across its collection of open and covered barges, raised wooden walkways, and floats, and usually Henny was around the place. Members used the little boat club in every season. They may, in fact, have needed to check their mooring lines or make sure their boats in dry dock were snugly covered. But the real draw was a hot potbelly stove in winter and a cold beer in summer and some conversation. Members who worked in factories stopped in at the end of their shifts. Self-employed men came in their trucks between jobs or at lunchtime. Conversation centered on the river. In January, had the icebreaker come through the channel? In summer, had the dredging barge gone by? How were the shad running in the spring? Whose boats were damaged in an autumn hurricane? How many blue-claw crabs had been netted? The river was the town square for many people, and Henny kept watch over it.

Henny was as solid on town history as he was on what had happened on the river that day. In Joseph Mitchell's essay "The Rivermen" (first published in *The New Yorker* April 4, 1959), Henny gives Mitchell a history lesson on the surname Ingold. William Ingold Sr. ran both the Edgewater Garage, at the foot of Hudson Avenue, and a shad fishing operation across River Road from the garage. In Mitchell's essay, Ingold is working on a car when he catches sight of Henny and the writer and says hi. After they've walked past, Mitchell asks Henny if Ingold is an old Edgewater name. In his characteristic mix of courtesy and authority, Henny answers:

> *Well, I should hope to think it is. It isn't one of the old Dutch names, but it's old enough, and Bill's got some of the old Dutch blood in him anyhow, through his mother's people. Knickerbocker Dutch ... Bill's mother was a Bishop, and her mother was a Carlock. The old Dutch blood came down to him from the Carlocks.*
>
> (582-3 of Up in the Old Hotel, Pantheon Books, 1992)

As rock solid as Henny's facts about the Hudson and life on its banks were, he was pulling my leg when I asked him the meaning of "Spuyten Duyvil." It's the name of a creek among the waterways that meet in the southernmost part of the Bronx—the Harlem River, the Spuyten Duyvil Creek, the Harlem River Shipping Canal, and the Hudson River. My dad and his boat cronies called the whole confluence Spuyten

Duyvil, and they treated the tricky crosscurrents and whirlpools there with respect.

When I asked my question, Henny slowly wound up his pitch. "Well," he said, "there was once an old Dutchman whose friend bet him a load of *guilders* that he wouldn't swim across that water. It was a lot of money, but the Dutchman said no. Swimmers drowned in those currents. Well, his friend kept raising the bet, so he hemmed and hawed but finally decided to take his chances. So, [here Henny acted things out] he spit into his hands, rubbed them together hard, and said 'I'll swim it and spite the Devil.' And that's what he did."

Wikipedia now tells me that "Spuyten Duyvil" literally means "Spouting Devil" (*Spuitende Duivel* in Dutch), a reference to the strong currents there. Alternative translations are "Spewing Devil," "Spinning Devil," or, more loosely, "Devil's Whirlpool" or "Devil's Spate." Anyway you looked at it, it was hard water to cross. So, even though Henny had added some drama to his answer, he had still landed pretty much on the money.

When I think of Henny now, I smell tobacco, not the acrid cigarette smoke in my parents' car, but a rich raisiny aroma from the tobacco that Henny chewed. And when I picture his face, a bit of brown tobacco juice has always found its way into the furrows bracketing his mouth. Like most people, my mother was fond of Henny and saw well past that small lapse. "Even with tobacco stains around his mouth, Henny Gaul is a real old-school gentleman," she would tell me.

The respect must have been mutual. He gave her a tiny brass carriage clock that had belonged to his wife.

The clock is a lovely chiming thing just 5 ½ inches high including its handle. The frame is brass, but the sides are beveled glass, so, as a child, I could watch its gears turn after my mother wound it. And sometimes, after Henny died, it would chime even when it hadn't been wound.

Photo by Author

"Henny's here," my mother would whisper when it did, and the ghostly visit would make her smile at the memory of her gentleman guest.

In essence,

A true gentleman could have a dirty face.

Meet That First Storyteller

My mother was ready to be happy in Edgewater as soon as she got there in 1947. She loved the light off the river, the mile-long reach of the view from their apartment, and the twinkling New York skyline at night. Perched high on the third floor of a house halfway up the hill to the cliffs, the apartment was a welcome contrast to living below ground, which they had been doing because of my father's principles. They had spent the first 19 months of my life in a basement apartment. My father would not pay "key money" to get an apartment in the post-war housing shortage, so my uncle helped them move to the no-fee basement apartment my father found in Fairview. The bed of my uncle's pick-up truck held what furniture they owned and my mother, who had told no one but my father that she was pregnant. She rode on top of their stuff in the pickup bed.

The name Fairview does not describe anything she could see from their apartment.

Her dislike of the place was strong enough that she gave up on the name she had picked if she had a girl, Linda. An upstairs neighbor had a daughter by that name and yelled it out into the backyard often enough that my mother came to associate it with life in the detested basement.

"I found mold growing on Daddy's dress shoes in the closet!" she'd tell me, still outraged years later. "It was not healthy there."

After finding the mold, she put her foot down. It was late 1947; surely, by now, they could find a better place. The dampness and darkness weren't aesthetic problems for my mother; they were, instead, matters of life and death. To be exact: her death and my abandonment. Too dramatic? No, life had taught this hale and hearty woman a dark fear: death came often and easily. And since, in 1946, she was 38 having her first child, many people, including her obstetrician, were not encouraging. "What do you expect at your age?" was his standard answer to any complaints she had. She was made to feel like she was doddering towards her delivery date.

How much death had it taken to frighten the cheery, uncomplicated child she had been? A good bit, but the first was the worst.

Olga, my grandmother; my Aunt Mim; Herman, my grandfather; my Aunt Helen; my mother, Elsa
Author's Photo

When my mother was 9, her 42-year-old mother died of tuberculosis. Common thinking about the disease in 1917 blamed the victim: TB sufferers were dirty, lived in slums, and were promiscuous. So added to the loneliness of the loss was the loneliness of a secret cause of death that couldn't be revealed.

The loss was vivid to my mother even when I was a girl, and she told me about it with a storyteller's instinct. In the years right after my grandmother died, my mother told me, she would sometimes see a woman in the street who looked, from behind, like her mother. A wild joy would fill her as she ran to catch up—"she's *not* really dead" —but it was always a stranger, and the little girl who became my mother always went home alone. The story moved me to tears when I was a child. I could feel her blossoming joy and her bleak disappointment. My own mother was sitting next to me as she spoke, but I was that child running down the street after a phantom.

In another story, she took me with her to the edge of my grandmother's grave. "We each had to pick up a clod of dirt and throw it down onto her coffin. Me and my sisters, all six of us, and my father, too. *Thump, thump, thump*, over and over," she said. "That sound of dirt hitting a coffin is so final." I could hear it and feel it 48 years later.

Next, when my mother was 14, her 19-year-old sister also died of tuberculosis. Mabel was her favorite sister and a wild child. Talking about her spunky personality always made my mother smile. At 15, Mabel tried to run away and join the circus. At 16, she married her boyfriend, a bus driver. At 17, she gave birth to a baby girl she named Frances. By 19, she was dead—for my mother, more loss and more secrets to keep. And another little girl left with no mother. My mother quit school at the end of 8th grade, she told me, because they hadn't given her the basketball letter she'd earned. But I suspect school just didn't move the scale when weighed against events in the rest of her life.

Eighth-Grade, School #6, 1922, West New York, NJ
My mother is third from the left in the last row

Author's Photo

Almost as an afterthought, when she talked about Mabel, my mother would add that her brother-in-law, the bus driver, had accidentally run over and killed a good friend. Tony and his friend, a "nice little man" my mother called him, had a game they played when they spotted each other while Tony was working. The friend would pretend to run in front of the bus Tony was driving. One day, they fatally miscalculated.

By the time she was 16, my grandfather had remarried. She didn't particularly like his new wife, but she did like her new stepsister. I have a studio photo of the four of them—my mom and grandfather, Edith, and her daughter, Ethel—posed stiffly in dress clothes in an open car. Not long after the photo was taken, Ethel died of spinal meningitis.

When my mother was 17, that stepmother, whom she liked even less by then, was crushed by a truck. As was the custom, her body was laid out in their living room. My grandfather then went out with some men he knew for drinks and sympathy, leaving my mother and her 19-year-old sister to watch over the corpse. No visitors showed up. It must have been a very long night.

My grandfather; his second wife, Edith; my mother; her stepsister, Ethel

Author's Photo

When my mother reached 20, her 29-year-old sister died of tuberculosis, too. She had lost her mother and two sisters to the disease in 11 years. Her stepsister and stepmother had also died in that time. So many women's deaths in one family.

So many daughters left behind ...

My Aunt Mim; Mabel's daughter, Frances; and my mother

Author's Photo

These dead women and their daughters crowded around my mother as she held me, a newborn girl, in her arms. It was hard for her to be hopeful for us. And she was 38 years old—"old for a first-time mother," her obstetrician told her at every checkup. Her happiness at my arrival was mixed with a presentiment of loss and with sadness. She was a big, healthy woman who'd delivered a big, healthy first baby in four hours, but she couldn't believe we would see each other through to my adulthood.

My mother and I, 1946

Author's Photo

I remained an only child, and we were too close. When I was young, any boundary I felt between us caused me anxiety. Amoeba-like, I had taken in her fear that we would lose each other. When I sat on her lap, I would lay my head against her chest to make sure that her heart beat. I was anxious when we were apart for more than just a school day. I passed my one trip to summer camp—after fifth grade--awash in homesickness so bad that I couldn't poop for the whole week. A feeling that she might not be okay filled my time in the woods. How could I know if she was still there when I couldn't see her? The sadness peaked on a hike when I could see the Hudson River far below the trail we were walking. The river led south to my mother; summer camp felt like exile. At the end, I walked away from the YWCA bus relieved and happy again. My father called me "the mustard plaster." That's how close I stuck to her. I had to.

Some 50 years passed before I could produce a dream that let me feel finally and fully clear about the sadness and worries my mother and I shared. That dream raised the images I needed in a story I could understand. Three characters were in it. I felt each one vividly, but in the dream, I look out from the eyes of a 16-year-old self on whom weighs a hard knowledge:

> *The scene we walk through is a generic suburban office park, leafy and anonymous. My mother has a medical appointment in one of the brick buildings. "Stay out here with your sister," she tells me and turns and walks away. My little sister is 10 or so, and she starts running up a hill to play as directed. "You always do everything Mom says to do," I tease her in a little bit of teenage pushback. So, to prove me wrong, she turns around and runs toward the building our mother has entered. It's then I remember that our mother is with a doctor discussing her recent diagnosis, which is terminal. I panic. I can't let my little sister find out that our mother is going to die soon. I follow her, arguing that I was wrong and pleading that we take a walk. But I can't get her to come back. She will find out that our*

mother is dying, and the grief that unfolds among us all will be my fault.

The characters acted out feelings I had wandered among for years, a complex dance of innocence, loss, grief, responsibility, independence, and selfhood. The loving mother will be snatched away. The independent impulses of the teenage girl put everyone at risk. The young child will be overwhelmed by the grief of abandonment. The dream had no neat ending; my relief came from recognizing the characters and accepting them all as parts of my feeling self. My path through adolescence to reach that dream was long and rough.

* * *

A fear that starts in early childhood is a chaotic fear because it predates the tools of reason and language. No coherent images or syntax are available then to make sense of its unfathomable darkness. On and off over the years, a dark form would inexplicably loom up in me, devoid of detail but full of the energy of fright. All the way to adulthood, this seemingly random fright accompanied me. It felt like the threat of madness.

* * *

> *Anxiety (loneliness or 'abandonment anxiety' being its most painful form) overcomes the person to the extent that he [sic] loses orientation in the objective world. To lose the world is to lose one's self, and vice versa; self and world are correlates. The function of anxiety is to destroy the self-world relationship ...*
>
> *(Love and Will by Rollo May, W. W. Norton & Company, 1969, p. 152)*

* * *

My mother's sunny outlook was what the rest of the world saw. The fear she focused on her and me we shared privately. She laughed readily at silliness, her own or others', until tears ran down her face. She enjoyed people and welcomed them to her home and her table. She spun stories that showed the world to be an interesting place and people its most interesting creatures. For the holidays, she baked hundreds of cookies. She loved feeding people. She sang off-key and with gusto in the car (for some odd reason, often the Cornell *alma mater*). "This, too, shall pass," was her mantra when difficulties occurred, and she successfully soothed many friends and family members with it. And most confounding, although it frightened me whenever she was sick in bed, I don't remember her worrying aloud when I was sick. I seemed to have taken in her fear across our skins.

"Your mother was wonderful," cousins and friends still tell me 35 years after her death. She was life affirming, nurturing, and jolly. She was compassionate. And she loved me dearly. Those aspects of her helped me survive when fear finally overwhelmed me.

Domestic Topography

Rivers of gravy and red sauce
Wind around potato and pasta mountains.
Cataracts of soup
Boil past cliffs of sliced bread.
Foaming gray surf
Scours linoleum, tile, and wood.
Miles of stitches lay
Across dresses, coats, and doll clothes.
Highways to family celebrations
Are paved with cookies, cakes, and pies.

Springs of bubbling coffee
Restore the spirits of guests.
A cave forms of lap and arms,
And hides a child in safety and peace.
The forces that shape the landscape
Do not fail
Until my mother's laughter has been stilled.

The Further Adventures of Lynn and Claire

Claire and I are hiding among the flowers and leaves of a huge wisteria vine. The vine winds around a cable that runs along stairs from my street up to hers. The wisteria plant is so old that its trunk has grown to the thickness of a man's bicep. Its clusters of lavender blossoms hide us from passers-by and fill our noses with a smell like grape soda. On this day, we are up in the vine spying on a neighbor boy, surnamed Gibbons, who is three or four years older than we are.

"A gibbon is a kind of monkey," Claire says, and we explode in giggles. Claire has been looking through the dictionary lately. Yesterday, she told me that there is a word called "hemidemisemiquaver" in music. I don't believe that, even though she has now mastered "Fur Elise" on the piano and therefore is more of a music expert than I am. But I read a lot, and to me that word sounds like junk parts screwed together.

Our game of hiding and spying gives us a little bit of power over older kids. People do things when they think no one's watching. Young Gibbons, for instance, is picking his nose, and we save that fact for future use. Someday we'll lob it at him like a dirt clod. The bigger kids hate this game, and they hurt us if they catch us. I lose half my freckles after one rubs poison oak on my face. Another pulls Claire's hair so hard he raises a bump on her head. But it's so much fun to make them explode, and sometimes we can outrun them. Claire's the fastest girl in our class, and the gym teacher picks me to somersault in the air on Parents' Night. We are strong little girls.

Kindergarten is long past, and we're regulars at each other's houses. Claire's father calls me "Carrot Top," which I hate from anyone else but not from him. He says it because he likes me, not to make fun of me. It feels like a hug. At Claire's house, I can have all the pretzels and potato chips I want. They're delivered in five-gallon tin cans with a lady in a sunbonnet on them. Bon Ton. My mother never buys chips or pretzels. And at Claire's house, there's the empty upstairs apartment to play in, where no one ever bothers us. It's our ship, our forest cabin, our island, our outlaw hideout. Heroic struggles to survive are played out up there before I have to go home for supper.

At my house, Claire gets only-child treatment, and she likes it. Her lunch order is taken, and the sandwich she asks for shows up with a pickle on the side. Anything in the refrigerator is up for grabs; no need to leave the last ripe peach for her brother. I even have a little TV in my bedroom, where we can watch shows curled up on the quilted spread of my double bed. When no grownups are home at my house, we make secret phone calls: "Is your refrigerator running?" "Yes." (Barely suppressed laughter.) "Well you better go catch it." We find especially hilarious our calls to an unfortunate woman in Fairview, a Mrs. Pepe, whose name we pronounce "pee-pee."

The hours of childhood pile up in heaps around us. Each day adds something shared: a joke that makes us laugh until our eyes run, a favorite candy bar and a serious debate about the best order in which to eat its layers, tidbits of gossip we overhear the grownups trading, a bologna sandwich bartered for a peanut-butter-and-jelly one at school. Some afternoons we sneak up the cliffs to tease the guard-dogs at mobster Albert Anastasia's house. We confess our sins at church on Saturday afternoons ("I took the Lord's name in vain." "I talked back to my parents." "I missed mass.") and share cherry Cokes and English muffins at the Plaza Drugstore after Sunday communion, when we are once again ready to meet eternity with sins forgiven.

Snow

As a kid on the streets of Edgewater, my connection to its seasons is physical and intimate. Their play on my senses signals changes in life that often suffuse me with joy. Smoke floats up from leaf piles in chill autumn air, its smell promising stew for supper and hissing apartment radiators. Each fall, I am a newly minted person—a fourth grader now or a sixth grader, not the infant I was in June. Later, in the sweetness of spring, petals fall from the ornamental cherry trees as I get off the school bus at George Washington School. In early summer, thunderstorms jolt the town with noise and lightning flashes. After the downpour, steam rises from the wet asphalt as I shiver in drenched shorts and shirt.

But the best season is winter because it brings snow. I feel a rush of surprise at the magic snow performs. A foot of glitter falls from the sky and costumes the worn old town like a queen. I stop just outside the front door, sniff the clean air, and savor the sunlight bouncing off a layer of snow that muffles everyday sounds. As children, we are allied with the snow's power to shut school and delay homework. Every blizzard is a victory for us.

My father is the rare adult who still loves snow, and I love having him to myself for an evening adventure. After supper, we put on heavy wool coats, wool snow pants for me, rubber boots, lots of socks, and we walk to the Public Service bus lot. The lot covers a chunk of town from River Road to Undercliff Avenue and from Hudson Avenue to Dempsey. A bus barn is on the property, but everything else is open grassy space that runs downhill toward the river. After the buses are garaged for the night, only sled traffic moves across it.

On our small adventure, my father and I enter the early darkness of a winter evening, walk up Hudson Avenue to Undercliff, and turn left. Now the excited voices of children can be heard calling out from the hill. A block farther on, we climb over a rail fence and wait our turn at the top of the lot. When a clear path opens on the crowded hill below, we sit down on my Flexible Flyer. He sits in back, holds the clothesline "reins," and rests his boots on the steering bar at the front of the sled. I sit safe between his knees, my smaller rubber boots between his.

Someone is always behind us to give a push. I feel the sled tip over the lip of the hill … and suddenly we are moving fast and free down across the lot toward the river below. Snow flies up from the runners and stings my eyes, but I try hard to keep them open in spite of the sting because all the lights of New York City are hurtling toward me, streaking up and down like fireworks with every bump we take. I am flying and I am safe. With my father behind me on the sled, I reach speeds I would never dare to by myself. As the lot flattens out at the bottom, we slide to a halt, roll off the sled, grab the rope, and get out of the way of the next riders. The slow climbs back up the hill bracket the brilliant speed in between.

In later years, I go sledding by myself at night, but my father sometimes joins me when I go ice-skating. Every winter, the town floods an outdoor basketball court next to the river and builds a bonfire in a big stone pit nearby.

I am no longer my father's tiny passenger, and these outings can be complicated. My father tries to teach me how to glide smoothly forward and backward on my skates the way he can. I have his attention and patience for one attempt. Then, "You're not trying," he says and skates away. I have been trying, and he says I'm not. We can't both be right. Some inner coherence fractures for me. I skate off with a friend, suspecting that my father was unfair, but the shame I feel for "not trying" is stronger than that suspicion and supports him, not me. Doubt about myself elbows in, and discouragement comes with it.

Estuary 1: Brackish Water

Technically, brackish water contains between 0.5 and 30 grams of salt per liter, which is a specific gravity of between 1.005 and 1.010. Thus, brackish covers a range of salinity regimes and is not considered a precisely defined condition. (Wikipedia)

Brackish: neither salt nor fresh but saltier or fresher.
A relative quality
Whose blurry margins in the estuary
Are in constant flux.
Brackish: neither here nor there but leaving here or almost there.
A relative position
Whose trip through the estuary
Is deflected, propelled, hindered, and drawn on
By forces both subtle and apparent.
What is saltier
Must slide over and into
What is fresher
And withdraw
And arrive again and withdraw again.
It cannot refuse to move
Among the million possibilities.
This is freedom.
This is chaos.

PART TWO
MIDSTREAM

My dinghy, Me 2, towed by my dad's speedboat

Author's Photo

Estuary 2: Out of the Mud

> *River estuaries form important staging points during the migration of anadromous and catadromous fish species, such as salmon, shad, and eels, giving them time to form social groups and to adjust to the changes in salinity. ... Besides the species that migrate through estuaries, there are many other fish that use them as "nursery grounds" for spawning or as places young fish can feed and grow before moving elsewhere.* (Wikipedia)

The anchor is stuck
In the mud of the river bottom.
My father pulls on the line
And pulls again
Then takes off his shirt
And dives from the bow of our boat
To follow the anchor line down
Into the cloudy green water.
Barely a minute passes
(*He'll die down there*. I panic.
Will his body float back up?)
Before the surface breaks around his face.
He pulls himself up into the boat.
The Danforth anchor is in his right hand,
And blood is streaming from his left.
In the dark, silky mud,
Something sharp lay hidden.

I, Me, My, Mine

A baby focuses its eyes, and the marvels of the world become clear and compelling. Soon its mouth and ears and fingers and the full expanse of its satiny skin are taking in whatever helps to solve the puzzles all around it. The young child continues that exploration of the world. But an adolescent's attention turns insistently inward. For her, fixation on some inner worry is like the sun rising in the east, a bear with hair, or a Catholic pope. What can she possibly accomplish with the blunt instrument she finds herself to be? "I" dominates the narrative when adolescence heaves into view.

Reading

In the 1950s in Edgewater, the air-conditioned library building is a refuge for me. On most silent, shimmering July and August afternoons, I leave our hot apartment and walk around the corner and up the hill to the library. Its formal Ionic pillars signal to me that books matter, and I agree. After my parents, books are the most important things in the world to me. In the summer, I visit the library so often that I zip through my Vacation Reading Club quota of book reports in less than a month. It's cool inside the building and quiet. In this sanctuary, I shed boredom and loneliness.

The world is lined up on its shelves for me to explore. Some days I walk up and down the aisles scanning the bookcases for possibilities. A biography of Queen Elizabeth I. Volcanoes. The mystery of Amelia Earhart. Sacajawea. A boy and his pet fawn. I pounce on whatever catches my eye. On other days, pursuing some interest I have, I go first to the card catalogue, where the brass fittings wink at me under the ceiling lights.

I read hundreds of books. I enter each one and live there for a while, and I am always startled to find myself still me at home when the pages run out. I talk to no one about the books. For my teachers, a plot summary is enough for a book report. The sizes, shapes, and colors of the ideas the stories leave behind in me are not what the grownups are looking for.

Edgewater Free Public Library

By Hisland7—Own work, CC By-SA 3.0
https://commons.wikimedia.org/w/index.php?curid=5997731

Miss Bowman, the librarian, enforces age-appropriate access. Graduation to the Young People's section is a milestone for me, but I quickly run out of interesting books there, and the Adult shelves are off limits. So I add another kind of reading to my program, a more exciting kind. My parents get three Sunday newspapers, and, at first, I just read the comic sections. With two of them—*The Journal American* and *The Newark Star Ledger*—I never get beyond the funnies. But the *Herald Tribune* describes a New York world of experiences and ideas that draws me in. Sometimes I need a word explained, so I read the *Trib* with a dictionary next to me on the floor. Some of the vocabulary I develop is inappropriate for my age, but I have enough sense not to use it. And my interest lies in more than the exciting, private words I look up. Through the *Trib*, I look out my front windows to the other side of the river and imagine richer lives. The Book Section especially broadens my tastes.

For Christmas, I ask for not only *The Lives of the Saints* and *The Littlest Angel* but also for a Penguin book on yoga and for Jack Kerouac's *Lonesome Traveler*. My mother, who reads magazines and newspapers, not books, takes my list to a card store in Cliffside Park. The store stocks a small selection of books that she hopes might cover the list, and she hands my requests to the shop owner.

Jack Kerouac
Moviestone Collection Ltd/
Almay Stock Photo

"How old *is* this kid?" the man at the counter asks after looking at the list.

"Fourteen," she answers.

He raises his eyebrows.

He has only *The Littlest Angel*, so she buys that and hands the rest of the list over to my aunt. This older sister works in Manhattan, where bookstores carry anything I can come up with, and my aunt gets the books for me.

Over Christmas vacation, I try out yoga postures and develop a good lotus and a respectable headstand. I wallow in tears over martyred Catholic saints and over the little boy who becomes an angel but needs his box of grubby treasures from Earth. Kerouac I read dry-eyed and with close attention. A chapter titled "Piers of the Homeless Night" opens his somersaulting narrative with a dock scene so familiar I can smell the river.

Back and forth across America I travel with his cast of eccentrics. Big drinkers. Voracious readers. All-night talkers. Restless men who ride the rails as my father had in the 1920s and freighters as he had in the '30s. When I travel with Kerouac, I keep my dictionary nearby, and my private vocabulary grows. But more subversive than those words are Kerouac's stories and his ideas that blow like gusts of wind through my mind. He warns me that people who do not like those ideas are everywhere.

The Further Adventures of Lynn and Claire

Claire has breasts. I can't ignore the fact. We are shopping for new bathing suits, and the one-piece Jantzens that I have been pulling off the rack are boring, unlike the two-piece suits that Claire is trying on. I'm shooting for a trim, athletic look. It's a low bar, but it's the best I can pull off with AA cups. At least my mother will like it.

I sense with dread that Claire will choose not just a two-piece but the gold two-piece with fringe all over it. She's wearing it now, standing in front of the mirror shaking herself from side to side and watching the fringe swing.

"This is it," she says then grins and ducks back into the dressing room.

I buy a nothing-special Jantzen in pale blue and white stripes. How wonderful it would feel to expect to be noticed and admired. Or, if not that, then to be invisible. This stupid suit will do neither. I will be seen, and I will be of little interest, and that will hurt. These days when I feel hurt and helpless, I get mad. I don't want to wear this bathing suit; I want to tear it to pieces.

... A Month Later

School is over when the summer heat hits and Claire and I make our first trip up the hill to Palisades Amusement Park. A matchbook with a PAL head printed on it gets us into the park for free. We have enough of these matchbooks to cover the whole summer. All we need is money for a Coke and French fries, and we can spend a day next to the big salt-water pool.

The air is still cool when we arrive at 10. There's plenty of room on the two sand beaches, but we never sit there. The little kids and their mothers do. Instead Claire and I spread our towels on the wooden deck behind the diving boards. Not many people are here, and it's so quiet we can hear the hum of the wave machine under the fake waterfall. Beyond the cyclone fence at the edge of the deck, the Palisades drop off sharply, and, far below, the Hudson shines flat under the climbing sun.

Wikipedia

Both of us pull bottles of Coppertone from our beach bags. As we slather ourselves and help with each other's backs, we glance sideways toward the diving boards. Next to the low board is the lifeguard's chair, and all the girls on the deck always hope that Franny will be working. He's handsome, clean-cut and blond. He's older than us and he has muscles, not like the wimpy boys in our class. And there he is! We catch each other looking at him and giggle.

We put on sunglasses and stretch out on our towels. The smell of Coppertone blankets the deck in the growing heat. Coppertone and chlorine, French fries cooking in peanut oil, and, in the evening, Noxzema spread over our sunburns. These are the smells of summer that tell us there is all the time we need in a day and we can spend it pleasing ourselves. The school year has ebbed and life is warm and sleepy and vast. More people arrive, but the rising noise level barely brushes against our sleepiness.

＊＊＊

When I open my eyes, Claire is gone. That's odd. Did she go to eat? But it's still early. I push up onto my forearms and sleepily scan the scene. No Claire at the food stand. No Claire in the pool. No Claire on either diving board. Maybe she went back inside to the locker? Then I see her. She's standing next to the lifeguard's chair smiling up at Franny, who seems to be saying something to her. He's smiling, too.

"I'm not leaving at 4:30," Claire says when she comes back to our towels.

"But we're supposed to be home by 5," I remind her.

"Franny gets off at 5. He's taking me on the rides."

"Your mom will be mad."

"She'll get over it."

Claire takes off her sunglasses, rolls onto her stomach, and closes her eyes.

Some girls can put on a two-piece bathing suit and, next thing, they've got a date with a lifeguard. The magic of breasts is powerful. I don't have that magic, and that difference between us will mean that I won't have Claire anymore. It's embarrassing: I feel like I'm peering in a window at her. The day falls flat. So I say good-by, and she just grunts. Walking back down Route 5, I'm moving back into the past, away from a larger world and back to just my mom, my dad, and me. For the first time since kindergarten, Claire is a tiny figure on the horizon. The distance is alarming.

"You're home early," my mother says as I walk into the kitchen.

"Yup."

I keep on going straight through the room.

"Want something cold to drink?"

"Nope."

Then I'm safely out of the kitchen and beyond her sympathy, which would make things worse. I close my bedroom door and look at myself in the big mirror over my dresser. Hopeless. Then I pick up a comb and, with its teeth pointing down, hit the dresser hard over and over. The edge of the dresser has lots of tiny holes in it; I've done this before. Once the anger is exhausted, I can cry.

Sons and Fathers, Daughters and Fathers, and What's on the Bottom of My River

Louis B. Litterine, Sr., my grandfather
Author's Photo

"You have to dig deep to bury your daddy." In the 1970s, a newspaper colleague wrote that at the beginning of one of his columns and added that it was a gypsy saying. I don't know if it is Romany, but I know it's correct about parents and children. Parents mean more to us than we can easily work with. The effort needed to transcend our relationships with them is intense. I don't think of that effort as burying, however; I think of it as facing the creepy stuff that sinks to the bottom of a river or an unplumbed mind. That stuff can never sink deeply enough to not hurt us, so we find ourselves forced to excavate it to survive.

In adolescence, I was negotiating womanhood with both the father in my head and the father across the kitchen table from me. The negotiations were tricky. My father was deeply loving and deeply wounded. Love made him vulnerable and wounds made him self-protective. If it took a harsh word to keep me at a tolerable distance, he delivered one. "All right, Sarah Bernhardt," was his standard warning that I was putting out too much feeling. It didn't matter whether that feeling was happiness, anger, or sadness. It was simply more feeling than he wanted to deal with. When old hurts pained him, he withdrew without explanation and required a wide space all around. "Don't bubble over around your father," my mother would warn me then.

My father and I, 1946
Author's Photo

Some of his hurt was standard working-class immigrant damage of the time: tough parents whose own harsh upbringing had made them harsh; too much hard work too early in life; a narrow view of what a man should be; and damage to a lively intelligence by *who-the-hell-do-you-think-you-are*. When unassimilated pain reared up, some blue-collar men eased it with alcohol. They missed supper, got home late from work, and went straight to bed to sleep it off. Then they got up at six the next morning and went back to work. My grandfather did that and my father did that. They were tough men who stifled feelings and did what they thought they had to do.

Here's a for-instance: One year my dad's family made a pet of the turkey they planned to eat on Thanksgiving. She was bought as a chick, named Genevieve, fed and watered, and allowed the run of the yard. I have photos of her grown into a big white gobbler. The family terrier, Cookie, was her friend. They hung out together in the yard and were the security patrol. A territorial turkey can be as protective as a terrier, and their combined voices—and Genevieve's flapping wings—frightened off strangers.

Author's Photo

When the inevitable happened and Genevieve was served on Thanksgiving Day, the family fled the table. Only my father and grandfather remained seated. Even Cookie whined and left the room when offered meat. But it was senseless to waste food, and my father and grandfather didn't let sentiment get in the way of doing what was sensible. So they ate her, silently except for the clink of forks and knives on plates, just the two of them. I assume it was one of them who had to kill her, maybe my father, in spite of how much he enjoyed the company of animals. He found them easier to deal with than people, more straightforward and less hurtful.

Our parakeet was his buddy when I was a little girl. The pale blue bird was allowed to perch on the rim of his glass at supper and sip his milk. My dad taught the bird, Porky Pig, to pull a Lucky Strike out of the pack in his shirt pocket and lift it to his lips when he sat in his easy chair at night. Eventually he taught the bird to cackle, "Give us a kiss, kid!" The two of them followed that with smooching noises. Once, outside a friend's cabin, I saw him hold a small bowl of seeds in the air for as long as it took to lure chickadees out of the woods. When they perched on the rim of the bowl, he watched them with a grin as they ate. And at that same cabin, he would draw chipmunks along the ground to him the same way. He would lay out a trail of seeds along the porch and hold the last seed between his fingers. He could sit still a long time until a chipmunk ate its way down the line of seeds. When it finally grabbed that last seed, he would rotate the seed very slowly while the preoccupied chipmunk hung on to it. Once the tiny animal was on its back, still clutching the seed, my father would gently rub its belly. It must have been hard to kill and eat Genevieve.

My dad began to work for my grandfather, a stonemason, when he was in kindergarten. On each walk home from school, he was expected to carry two river stones for the fireplace in the house my grandfather was building for the family. At sundown, my dad also lit black oil lamps, the kind that look like cartoon bombs, to warn people around my grandfather's fresh cement work in town sidewalks. When he was older and sometimes worked full time for his father, Saturday evenings were when he was paid. Payment was an issue of control and could be a drawn-out process. My grandfather would keep him waiting for his wages at the kitchen table ... seven o'clock ... eight o'clock ... but even by nine o'clock, my father wouldn't have asked for his money. Finally, my grandfather would pay him, and he could go out with his friends. The standoff showed to each man's satisfaction who was stronger.

But make no mistake; my grandfather loved my father. He was his first son and his namesake. My father was gone for three years during WWII. On the mantel of that same fireplace he'd carried river stones for was his Army photo. He'd looked straight into the camera when the photo was taken, so his eyes followed you around the room. My grandfather would walk back and forth in front of the fireplace in tears. "He's watching me. He's watching me," he'd tell my mother. He missed him and he was afraid of losing him. My tough little grandmother, on the other hand, angry that all her sons and sons-in-law were fighting overseas, called cancer curses down on FDR; no tears for her, only revenge would be sweet.

I'm sure my grandfather never told my father that he loved him. Instead, he exercised his rough control. He needed and trusted control, so, like most parents, my grandfather loved my father as best he could.

My father was the first of seven siblings to survive, so he was also, as eldest brother, the point man. Picture my uncle and his new girlfriend leaving my grandparents' house after her first visit. It had been a nice afternoon eased along by homemade red wine and grappa. "That went well, didn't it?" she said with relief. But the most important nod had yet to come. "You haven't met my big brother yet," he told her. The younger six kids had been trained to this deference. My grandmother didn't threaten my aunts and uncles with "wait 'til your father gets home." Her last warning was always "wait 'til your big brother gets home." His two younger brothers were barely a year apart in age and looked like twins. They bonded tightly. My dad sat alone on a pinnacle of authority.

His curiosity also set him apart. He had a big old steamer trunk in the attic when I was a child. Its lining smelled inviting, a warm, whispery mix of faded fabric, dust, and old books. Rummaging in it was like rummaging in his long-ago thoughts. There were four volumes of *The Winning of the West* by Theodore Roosevelt. These were beautiful suede-bound books with covers of unbleached muslin, objects to enjoy even before opening them. He liked essays and, except for Charles Dickens, had little interest in fiction. In the old trunk were *Essay on the Freedom of the Will* by Schopenhauer; Emerson's Essays, a small dark green book with its title stamped in gold on the spine; and *44 Essays* by Christopher Morley, a gift from his favorite high school teacher, whose bookplate was still in it:

THIS BOOK BELONGS TO

HARRIET MEEKER

But for me, the best books in the trunk were my father's own journals and the notebooks full of his letters to my mother from during the war. He began the journals during high school summers when he worked in traveling carnivals or rode the rails from one sweaty, unskilled job to another. In Florida, he gets thrown out of the same small town for vagrancy three times in 24 hours. He's stabbed in Florida, too, but he never explains how it happened. In his reticence, he seems embarrassed.

My father on the road in the 1920s

Author's Photo

Later, in the 1930s, he wrote in journals during Merchant Marine voyages through the Panama Canal to the Northwest, to Africa, and as far as Madagascar. He describes with an engineer's precision his first trip through the locks of the great canal. But he also writes about a night in Seattle's redlight district that involved him and a buddy from the ship, two good-time gals, and a whole lot more alcohol than was good for any of them. He had a great time and happily reports that one gal "went fruit." Although he was a physically modest man, he never limited my access to his journals. Maybe he'd forgotten what was in them.

His descriptions of unimaginably far-off places opened out the world to me. He marveled at Africans who "file their teeth into points and live on mealy meal and raw fish rotted in the sun." The porters in Cape Town, he wrote, loaded freighters by climbing rope nets up the side of a ship, crates balanced on their heads. He proclaimed Mauritian women "the most beautiful in the world." He sketched ships' engines. And he wrote how, delirious and hospitalized with malaria, he missed his ship out of Mombasa. A gentlemanly period of recuperation followed that included lots of afternoon teas in the company of young Englishwomen.

My dad on a freighter
Author's Photo

On his voyages back home, he would write expectantly about seeing his family again. His thoughts were as sentimental as a greeting card. But within days on shore, he was drinking too much. Why? He doesn't explain; he just berates himself. Was feeling lonely at home harder than feeling lonely in a strange port? Had someone close to him hurt him?

Or did sheer boredom become overwhelming? Without comment, he just ships out again, usually sooner than planned, once on the night before his sister's wedding. His mother was furious.

He continued writing during the war in letters to my mother, whom he'd married in 1940. The stories are about military training, sweltering in Texas and knee deep in Montana snow. Then his letters came from overseas—North Africa and Italy. He was crew chief for a bomber, responsible for every nut and bolt in the beautiful machine. He loved that plane. Any problems it threw his way could be solved with his training and his patience. People were harder. Eventually, he vowed to make no more close friends. He told my mother that the pain was too much when a pilot, a navigator, or a bombardier came back from a bombing run in pieces, and my dad's crew had to hose out the fuselage. But he also managed to tell her funny stories. In Italy, he wrote, he got fresh apricots by banging a jeep into trees. The ripe fruit fell and filled the jeep, and my father took off fast before the shotgun-waving farmer could get across his orchard.

That laughing storyteller could completely disappear in the father across the kitchen table from me. At the table was a life-hardened man, too tired at night to read more than the newspaper, sometimes so tired he would fall sound asleep while stretching out his sore back on the living room floor as he waited for supper. He worked hard in a small river town next to the small town where he was born. His hands were so callused that he could not close his fists, but his body was of little consequence to him. It was another tool he used for work. That body was strong and hard. He never used it to hurt me, but I was scared of its latent power.

His great pleasure was the Hudson River. He rarely took vacations; there was always plumbing to do. But weekends were for riding in the speedboat he'd treated himself to. We'd anchor the boat and picnic on a wooded bank upriver, well beyond where most hikers got to in Interstate Park, and he'd grill spareribs or chicken or pork chops with his usual precision and patience. My fun-loving father showed up then, clowning in photos, making a willow whistle for me from the tree that shaded our rock table, and once showing me a nest of baby shrews on the riverbank. "Why are they wet?" I asked after stroking one. "They're not," he said. "Their fur is just so soft."

What constituted his pain he kept private, even from my mother. But when that pain erupted, he came home late and drunk. I felt ashamed of him then and disappointed. And I felt ashamed of myself for being so ineffective and so unimportant to him that I couldn't fix whatever was wrong. Eventually he seemed to prefer the child I'd been to whatever I was turning into. In my adolescence, we drifted apart and shared no more little adventures.

* * *

The father I'd come to know from his books and his journals in the attic trunk was a curious adventurer, a connoisseur of odd characters in strange places, a reader of difficult books, an explorer of big ideas, a romantic, and an idealist. He knew the world was putting on a great show just beyond the horizon. That father, I adored. But I had another father, one who withdrew and got drunk when he was troubled, one whose pain brought pain into my life, too.

The river keeps moving. You can ride it out to all the oceans of the world and all the adventures one lifetime can handle. But dangerous debris lies on its bottom, broken things, dead things, lost things. I found I could not easily float downstream above them all.

Poem for My Father's Birthday

On your birthday,
I will say
Much more
Than you.
I will talk into
The silence
Of you
Until it seems
That I
Talk too much,
Not that you
Are too silent.
Why do you make
Me drag you
Out of yourself
To me?
Why am I
An interruption of you?

Breath

I learned to stand apart from my body in junior high school, to look at it through other people's eyes. In childhood, I was my body. I ran only because it felt good to pound my legs against the ground and be fast. I ice-skated fast, too, because I could feel like the wind. I ate what tasted good without a second thought. I read until my eyelids sank over my books. And I danced wildly around the living room when my mother played her 78-rpm records. But in junior high, I began to look through boys' eyes and compare myself to other girls, and I was cruel. My feet, too big. My hair, too curly. My breasts, too small. My face, covered with freckles. My fingers, blunt with raggedy nails. My white eyelashes, invisible. I couldn't make much of my body, so I decoupled from it. Not that I understood that—I just felt increasingly like a stranger to myself and apart from the rest of the world. The alienation worsened the old issue of fear and breath. Home could get bleak enough sometimes to make my chest seize up, but school was becoming an unhappy place, too. At school, I monitored myself. But harder to bear than even the self-consciousness was an out-of-control teacher whose behavior teetered on a narrow ledge.

This troubled man put tacks in the walls to line our desks up with. Most mornings, at the end of homeroom, we thought we had aligned them perfectly and had met the first of the day's inscrutable adult demands. We would stand to line up for first-period class, but, after a moment of silence, he would grab a book and slam it with all his strength flat down on his desk. The sudden crash made us jump. "Now, line up the desks correctly!" he would yell. "They're half an inch off!" Some of the boys were tough and seemed unfazed by his screaming and his red face. But the sudden, bizarre outbursts terrified me. I was smart and always worked hard, so school had always been under my control and, therefore, a safe place. But throughout junior high, I was increasingly under his control instead, and by ninth grade, I spent three periods of every school day with him—homeroom; my Latin class, which dropped from 20-some students to five scared girls; and my French class, where I had more company but where he would suddenly screech "Sit up straight!" at one of the boys, and then, "Do you think this is funny?" when the offender smirked. Every year, we did a foreign language play for parents; then his power to frighten me stretched out into after-school rehearsals, when I should have been at home and free of him. By ninth grade, the third year of his fury, I often told my mother that I felt like I couldn't breathe and that I needed to stay home from school. She took me to the doctor, but I never told either of them what was frightening me. I missed many days of school that year but still got straight A's. My breathing miraculously recovered in June when junior high school ended.

An Alphabet of Guys

A Is for Awkward

(Because the soundtrack for adolescence is always rock and roll: *Blue Moon* by The Marcels)

There are two criteria for a first boyfriend: he has to be a boy and he has to be taller than you are. A is a boy, but I am taller than he is. We're in ninth grade, and I deal with the height issue by walking in the gutter when we're hanging out. After school, all along River Road, Route 5, Undercliff Avenue, I stick to the street and he stays on the curb. I have a boyfriend because I think I'm supposed to have one. Hormones haven't even kicked in yet. It's all theoretical. We're following a script learned from books, songs, TV shows, and movies. Its point is the audience. How do A and I look to our audience?

Well, with me walking in the gutter, we do not look cool. Plus I'm not shapely. I do not dance well. And I get good grades—I can't help it. A is, as mentioned, shorter than I am. That's what I know best about him. I think about it a lot.

What do we talk about when we walk around town after school? Apparently nothing much that matters because it will be decades before I learn that his father sometimes beat him. And I don't tell him about the sadness in my life when my father drinks, how my family veers off course then and later veers back on course, and how I struggle to see what causes either change.

So, what do A and I talk about? That's the wrong question. The question is do we talk at all. The answer is no. Like icebergs, most of who we are is below the surface, unknown to both of us and out of our control. That ignorance fosters casual cruelty. Before our junior high school graduation dance, he drops me for a better-looking prospect, who then does not show up. I go to the dance with the son of one of my mother's friends. Then I turn around and ditch my date for his better-looking cousin. Although the relationships are theoretical, the hurts are not.

B Is for Belonging

(Soundtrack: *In the Still of the Night* by The Five Satins)

My social life changes overnight after junior high school. Literally overnight. Like some fairy tale weirdly set in New Jersey. On the last day of summer vacation in 1961, I'm a solitary outlier who's home with my parents at night. The closest I get to parties are the prank calls to my house from the partygoers in my class. Labor Day 1961 passes like most days and gives not a clue of what's about to happen. But on the very next day, I'm sitting in study hall in a new school, and a boy is flirting with me. He's cute, he's taller than me, and he's flashing a nice smile. I'm not the agent of this abrupt change in my life. I'm the same girl I was the day before. This state of grace descends simply because Edgewater is too small to have a high school. Instead, we're sent to Leonia after ninth grade.

Within days, I have new girlfriends. Within weeks, I have a steady boyfriend. I'm on the phone every night. I go to parties on weekends. At lunchtime, I smoke and chatter with my friends on the golf course across from the high school. The teachers challenge us with interesting ideas and don't care how our desks line up. My classes are no longer struggles with stupefying boredom. I study hard and I socialize hard. I don't get on the Edgewater bus after school. Instead, I spend almost all my time in Leonia. I'm at club meetings or hanging out in the halls at school or at friends' houses. Often it's dark by the time I get on the No. 1 bus to go home. Sometimes I have supper at my boyfriend's house; then his father drives me home.

This boy's attraction is not theoretical for me. Young and sweetly stupid we may be, but the joy is physical and real. Hormones have kicked in, and his nearness delights me. When his whisper brushes across my ear, my whole back shivers. I can feel the outline of the muscles when he puts his arm across my shoulder. Those arms are hard, and I like to look at the veins just below the skin where I see them twine like vines. They're insistent, not like the veins hidden in the soft, white flesh of my arms. The heat from our differences makes my head spin. Sometimes when we French kiss, his spit gets in my mouth, and I'm shocked to find it tastes good, like clean winter air or a fresh cherrystone clam. I love to press against the front of him when we slow dance: I'm seen and I'm wanted and it feels good.

While cops patrol the streets of Leonia and Edgewater, Palisades Interstate Park is ours. On dates, we park at dark overlooks on the cliffs above the Hudson. Most weekend nights the lots are packed with teenagers in cars doing what one radio DJ calls "watching the submarine races." We balance on a fine line, kissing, stroking, noticing each other's reactions, but we never fall off that line. It's a risk too far for the kind of kids we are.

Loneliness has eased. My friends and I are in constant, all-absorbing conversation. We talk on walks around Leonia. We chatter at our lockers as we change books between classes. We whisper in class, and, when we can't whisper, we pass notes. In the cafeteria, over macaroni and cheese and applesauce, we talk. As soon as we get home from school, we call each other and talk on the phone some more. We talk at parties. We talk about who likes who. About what we're reading. About the moods we're in. About movies. About clothes we want. About homework we have to do. About records, about teachers, and about our parents, the adults who have been the bedrock of our lives and are now something apart from us that we discuss. A gap has opened. On one side, our world, fully known only to us. On the other side, all that used to be. Parents sense the loss. In response, my father makes up silly nicknames for my boyfriend.

Girlfriends are telling each other everything for the sake of savoring what is happening in our lives and for the sake of feeling our closeness in shared secrets. Every step along the path of a romance is reported: the arm that slowly stretches across our shoulders at the movies, the hand that reaches for ours on the street, the kiss that lingers, the tongue that explores, and, finally for most of us, the hands that dance across our bodies or knead them, over clothes and under clothes, and our own hands that dance across and knead theirs. If anyone takes intimacy further, few of us know about it. Boys together by themselves are an unknown world. We suspect they tell scores, and we hope not about us. We want to have our cake and eat it, too.

* * *

My high-school romance lasts almost to graduation. What breaks it up is the sense that something more exciting is somewhere beyond the here and now. We're not conscious of the thought, but our world is ballooning out past these small towns, and, in September, we'll be moving on. The time I spend with B is a well-worn path. Nothing new gets said. Nothing new happens. I'm bored. He's bored. It's not fun anymore, and we can't shake things up. But we also can't let go and be alone. We're stuck and we're angry and we fight a lot. Eventually, we just wear the whole thing out and drive each other away. It's a stormy time for everybody; none of my friends graduates with a longtime romance.

At graduation, my time in high school sure looks successful, but I feel no agency. My life feels coincidental and not of my making. A disquiet is rising in me. I write in my journal:

> *What is it? that is not*
> *there as it was last year.*
> *I am waiting. I am*

*waiting for this thing as
I did not have to wait
for it last year.*

My growing anxiety leads to a need for more control. I've started eating in weird patterns to lose weight—no food for a day, next day one big meal, no food again the next day. But I'm *not* in control. And I feel a bleak suspicion that I will not be able to handle what lies ahead of me. That suspicion will be realized, and, for a while, the fright will tear me up.

C Is for Change

(Soundtrack: *Heat Wave* by Martha and the Vandellas)

One June night right after high school, a door slams shut as I leave the house. No one hears it, not even me because I haven't noticed the sense of purpose I'm packing. I've temporarily hidden even from myself the break I plan. I'm headed to an open-house party that will have no parents on the premises. It's billed as a girls' pajama party, but every teenager in small-town Leonia knows it will be a crowded, coed, open house. I take the Number 1 bus to Leonia then walk up the hill through a night that smells like cut grass. High school is over; anything is possible.

The party is at a big split-level house in a neighborhood with no sidewalks. The house is lit up like a cruise ship. All the front windows are closed, so only a low thump of bass reaches me from the record being played inside. I walk through an empty front yard, but out back, teenagers are all over the grass. Once I'm in the backyard, I can hear what the record is. It's *Heat Wave* by Martha and the Vandellas. I sit down on the ground with my back against a tree, light a cigarette, and scan the crowd for my friends.

I recognize the guy who heads toward me. We overlapped at school for a year before he moved away. He played basketball, one of the rumored stoners on a team of talented bad boys. I like basketball players. Their fast-moving ballet is the only school sport I watch with interest. So I'm glad when he lowers himself onto the grass next to me and says hi. His hair is blond and long enough to curl up under the edge of the Jeff cap he's wearing. His eyes are pale blue behind his wire-rim glasses. In time, I'd discover that nothing in the world was sexier than watching him take those glasses off. After they were gone, he would seem as vulnerable to me as I felt to him.

But I'm not there yet. For now, I'm enjoying the look of his mouth, a Cupid's bow that twists a little into a knowing grin. This angel looks cynical and kind of dangerous. While the story in my head is that I'm looking for true love and commitment, I suddenly know instead that *he's* just what I'm looking for, recklessness and risk.

"Got a cigarette?" he says.

"Sure." I hand him my pack of Marlboros.

"I saw you and your friend on Broad Avenue last week."

"I didn't see you."

"Pauly and I were up in Mr. Clark's room."

Mr. Clark is the boys' basketball coach, and players are always coming back to visit him at the high school after they've graduated.

"What day?"

"Friday afternoon."

"We were going to the city."

"You have such long red hair. You had it loose, and it was blowing around—it's beautiful."

An unexpectedly great start! So we talk. We've read and liked some of the same Beat poets. And he's read Kerouac, but not my favorite Kerouac, *Lonesome Traveler*. I like rock and roll, but I only confess to especially liking the Stones. I sense that confessing to the Beatles might be uncool. He thinks the Stones are okay for rock and roll, but he likes blues and rhythm and blues. He mentions some favorites. I have no idea who Little Walter or Son House is. We can agree on Dylan. And, yes, we both like basketball. All the while, I'm watching myself talk, scared I'll run out of things to say. That fear gets us into a bedroom sooner because I can't bear the anxiety that I might say something stupid during an empty silence. Except for "I love you" or "I want you," everything I say to him for two years will be to ward off that silence. I'll keep a script going. But he's a smart guy, and one day he'll ask me, "Why don't you believe anything you say?" Then I'll know that he sees me as I see myself and that it's over.

But for tonight, we're hormonal teenagers, and the house has empty bedrooms, so we grab one and lock the door. Then we hold ourselves against each other full length. To be alone together in a dark bedroom is a luxurious sensation. We kiss once. Twice. Three times. Soon his hands are at work along my spine undoing a long line of tiny buttons. "My mother made this blouse," I say in a moment of conversational bankruptcy. "Feels like your father did," he mumbles into my neck. I am being stolen out from under my father's protection. How wonderful!

Eventually all our clothes are off. He really is a beautiful boy, with slender hips and milk-white skin; I could eat him up whole. Other kids knock on the bedroom door—"don't bogart the room" —but we just laugh. The door is locked; it's up to us what happens next, and it's wonderful to be in bed together alone with no clothes on. I feel an exhilarating energy. I don't give a damn about anything for a change. But as time passes, we run into a bit of trouble. I'm a virgin, and he's surprised. "What about B?" he asks. "No," I answer. "Well … damn," he says.

We have fun anyway until the front doorbell rings. At the sound, he freezes and listens intently. A policeman has been sent to quiet down the party. C lifts the curtain just a little to peer out. "Shit! Officer Christmas," he whispers. "I have to get out of here." Apparently he shares history with this cop. He gets his clothes back on fast, slips out the bedroom door, and crosses the hall into a back bedroom. I hear him lift a window and crawl out through it, and he's gone.

I paw around in the dark getting my clothes off the furniture and the floor. I have never met a boy so exciting and so beautiful. I can't imagine why he noticed me, but he did, and I am in for the whole ride now.

* * *

Virginity's never lost. We all know exactly where we leave it. I leave mine in the grass behind the Methodist Church in Leonia. And I wait only 24 hours after meeting C to do that. Penetration's not a peak experience; I'm kind of dry. But the abstract magic of sex carries me along. I have plenty of stories I twine around sex to organize it in a way that pleases and reassures me. I'm just 18 and I'm full of stories.

Not a minute after we're finished making love and are quiet again, a cop car pulls into the church parking lot. The headlights slowly sweep toward the deep darkness that hides us among trees and bushes. We jump up and take off and we're lucky. The headlights don't catch us, although they easily could have because, while C's jeans are quickly up and he can run, I can only toddle. As I make my escape, I am trying to pull up a girdle that hugs my ankles. It's 1964, and no matter how skinny you are, you wear a girdle to look even skinnier. But I've just been half-naked on the grass with C and obviously have nothing left to hide. The girdle now seems especially stupid, and I'm cursing the big elastic band that hobbles my ankles.

"I am never wearing this goddamn thing again," I fume once I'm safely hidden. Then I throw the girdle into a huge hydrangea bush.

C is bent over laughing. I love that.

Leonia Methodist Church

The Collotype Co., Elizabeth, N.J.

Comedy, or more accurately farce, will always be a part of our romance because, when we meet, we are 18 and 19 years old. For the next two years, making love will be catch as catch can. I live with my parents when I'm not away at Elmira College in New York State. He lives, well, everywhere and nowhere—sometimes at college in Syracuse, sometimes with his parents, sometimes in Provincetown, sometimes in a friend's basement, sometimes in Chicago. This is not a steady relationship. He's in town. He's out of town. He's back in town.

For me, life shines only when C writes or calls or visits. His handwriting on an envelope concentrates my happiness like a magnifying glass. The possibility of his voice on the other end of the phone is the reason I pick it up. We make love where and when we can. When it's warm, we're outdoors under the night sky. The damp grass squeaks beneath us, and mosquitoes bite. One time, when I visit him at college, we're in a boarding house. And, because they're cheap and anonymous, we're in a boarding house again during the Newport Folk Festival. It's the year Bob Dylan goes electric. Purple lights shine over the stage as he starts rocking out, and the crowd splits between boos and cheers. I've come with girlfriends, but I keep an eye out for C wherever I go. On Saturday morning, when I finally see him coming down the beach, I run into the surf with my clothes on. See? I can be spontaneous and reckless! We take over my friends' boarding-house room later that night.

It's hard to believe that no adults realize what's going on with all of us that first summer after high school. We're running wild and getting away with outrageous lies. No one is using birth control; birth control's not romantic, not spontaneous. Who wants that kind of story? One night, four of us go to the Englewood Boat Basin. My girlfriend's father owns a small cabin cruiser docked there. From a payphone near the river, I call my parents and say I'm staying overnight at her house. She tells her parents she's at mine. You can hear that we're outdoors. Boat and river noise is in the background, but no parent challenges us. Now we have a whole night to spend with our boyfriends. She takes the back deck, hidden under the canvas boat cover. C and I are in the cabin on a narrow bunk. "I wish you'd get pregnant so we could get married," C says. "Yeah," I answer and I mean it. I'll see the passivity and the mooncalf stupidity in that exchange years later. At this point, we're 18 and 19 years old with no resources, but the possibility of marrying is thrilling and makes perfect sense to me.

The dance we do together is calibrated to never commit both of us at the same time. We pull each other close, and we shove each other away. The mixed signals confound communication. I adore him; I will not drop my guard. He wishes we could marry; he doesn't want me to count on him. I buy some black lace and tell him I have a surprise; "I hate surprises," he says. He calls from Chicago; I'm on a couch kissing a friend of his. I send him a "relationship" card; he writes back quoting Dylan, "to bring you flowers constantly and to come each time you call, it ain't me, babe." Then he adds, "Tear up all my letters … they are true only as I am writing them."

To me, he's the invulnerable, risk-taking adventurer I want but can't trust. What am I to him? I have no idea. I assume I mean less to him than he does to me. Even when in bed one night he says, "Too bad men and women don't come at the same time," I hear no vulnerability, no "Am I doing this right?" I'm, as always, worried that it's my fault … and kind of mystified, too. This is sex, right? This act and the stories I tell myself about it? I don't hear a 19-year-old boy who knows nothing about foreplay and clitorises. I don't hear the question he's asking me.

We're lucky, and I don't get pregnant. But I don't feel lucky because C's calls and visits get more and more occasional. Like a last breath, it's hard to know exactly when the end comes. Eventually, I hear he's heading to California. Some girl is going with him. It's clear as glass to me. The real me has been found out and found wanting.

Here my soundtrack changes to *It's All Over Now, Baby Blue*. I feel beaten up inside. I've never been open to this much hurt. Then a new feeling hits, and it's frightening. All that I know as me is disintegrating, and the loss feels infinite. I'm falling, and no ground rises to stop my descent. Everything has turned to rushing air. I think then that this is grief over C, but it isn't just that; the loss of self and the fright that follows have been waiting in me for a long time.

***

Years later, I can find material online that makes sense of what happened. The following short excerpts, for example, are from the much longer and more detailed and nuanced doctoral dissertation of Dr. Eugenia Cherkasskaya, a clinical psychologist in New York:

> *... psychoanalytic writers consider sexual desire as the unconscious wish to fuse with another and transcend the boundaries of self. As [O.F.] Kernberg [1995] asserts, the individual must be able to maintain the integrity of self in the face of such fusion and obliteration of boundaries between self and other. This suggests that the capacity for sexual desire requires the development of an autonomous identity and therefore successful achievement of separation and individuation. (21)*
>
> *... The difference between the mother and father becomes important in the conflict between separation and connectedness, and independence and dependence. [J.] Benjamin [1990] suggests that the father comes to represent freedom, separation and desire. (45)*
>
> *... Based on the conceptualization of sexual desire as the wish for merger with the other, the sexual act may be threatening to those who do not feel fully individuated and separate – threatening to their relationship with the mother and threatening to their integrity of self. (176)*
>
> (Cherkasskaya, Eugenia, "Re-Considering Female Sexual Desire: Internalized Representations Of Parental Relationships And Sexual Self-Concept In Women With Inhibited And Heightened Sexual Desire" (2014). CUNY Academic Works. https://academicworks.cuny.edu/gc_etds/317)

Threatening to the integrity of self indeed.

* * *

After enough tears and days of barely eating or of stuffing myself, I am steady enough to function. One day I go out and have most of my hair cut off. The hairdresser takes two cigarette breaks during my appointment. His hands are shaking. I think he's worried I might regret it. The cut is short and geometric, a cut Vidal Sassoon designed for Rudi Gernreich's models. A sharp point of hair descends in front of each ear. A larger point goes down my neck in back. At first, friends don't recognize me on the street. Good! Now I'm someone geometric and kind of artificial.

But chopping off my hair doesn't make a break with childhood, and it doesn't cure adolescent pain. I retreat. I change colleges and commute from home, so I'm living with my folks again. Most of my friends are away at school; I'm alone a lot. I seal up the troubled place inside myself and turn away from what's happened to me.

Reality Check

In the interest of accuracy, I provide here excerpts from the few letters C sent me in the years after he left for California.

First, a Christmas card with a pen-and-ink drawing of angels on the front. The message begins with some lines from *First Girl I Loved* by the Incredible String Band:

> " 'You've grown into a
>   female stranger
> and if I was near you
>   now
> I wouldn't be there at all.'

> … *This by way of a greeting, longtime Lynn. I hear about you once a year from Paul or Lois (recently) and wonder what you do and who. I figured you'd like this card anyway.*
> *Yours for Christmas and cherubim-bim, C"*

Next, a letter on loose-leaf paper. I'd been in rough shape, and a friend said C blamed himself, so I sent a note back west with her. By then, I was getting better, and I knew that what had shaken me had started long before I met him.

> *"I was pleased and surprised to get your message-letter … you're feeling nice and I'm glad. It was about the only up story I got from back east. The coast is really a different place. I think you'd dig it. There are piney woods here with heather*

like and sea spray ... However, girl, I hear your hair has not grown out! The world is lonely for your flaming head. I don't know if you got that Xmas card last year. I sent it (addresswise) like this ['near the Horseshoe Bend, o mailman, Edgewater NJ']. I hope you hear from me. This is a year that's never been before. ... Love and luck from your California moon crank, C"

And last, about a month before my birthday, a letter on plain paper that begins with a poem:

"When I was young
>   my friends & I danced
>>   crazy, drunk &
>>   rubber legged.
>   Now, one's in the navy;
>>   one's taken up with
>>   a bottle imp – and me
>   me? I'm so lonely I
>>   write poems.

If you do plan to ever come to California write ahead & I'll show you around. Also try to get you a place ahead. Get in touch with _____ at _____ and maybe she can get you a job at Grove Press where she works. Also say hello for me. You'll like her I know. C"

He'd enclosed a newspaper headline:

Mysterious Theft of Moon Dust

And on the back of the clipping, he'd written,

"HAPPY BIRTHDAY—THEY'RE GETTING CLOSER TO THE SANCTUARY, I FEAR—"

I read these messages years later searching for the flat-out rejection I'd felt when I was 22, but it's not there. What I can see is our old dance of come-close/get-back, and I can see it clearly now. The letters are what they always were; I've changed.

Subjunctive Mood

I could not understand
You
When you said
The vulnerability
Is the good part, the necessary part,
The part to trust.

The Further Adventures of Lynn and Claire

Our lives started to branch away from each other late in junior high school. Claire is invited to parties; I am not. I am not cool. My assumption is based on the evidence: I'm alone so I must be unwanted; I am unwanted so I must not be cool. Later, in high school, we lead even more separate lives—different friends, different classes, different plans for the future. I go on to college but attend in fits and starts, studying hard then quitting suddenly and coming back home, studying hard again then quitting suddenly again. Sometimes, when I'm home, I get a job, but it never lasts long; I quit. I can't seem to break free from my parents, from their house, and from the river town I used to love.

Claire does not go to college. She lives with her parents and works in a bank. She does her job for the salary; money's enough; she doesn't need to love her work. She buys a yellow Mustang with a white convertible top. She knows how to give it a tune-up herself. Most weekend nights, she's at a bar with friends. Different lives. But Claire still lives on the next block, and when I'm home, we sometimes take the same meandering walks around Edgewater we used to. We walk and talk and chain-smoke Marlboros. We've been friends for 16 years, so it's natural that when Claire decides to marry, I'll be a bridesmaid.

At a bar on the cliffs above the Hudson River, Claire meets a West Point cadet, falls in love over tequila shots, and will soon enter what I see, with envy, as a fully mapped adult life. They'll marry, and for the next 13 months he'll be in Vietnam. The Army will ship Claire, her yellow Mustang, and her piano to Hawaii, where she'll live. After that, they'll go on deployments together, overseas Claire hopes.

She's looking for some adventure. Once his obligation to the Army is over, they'll leave the military. Claire finds long-term regimentation hard to take.

The wedding is in the Cadet Chapel at West Point on a chilly autumn Sunday when the Hudson lies still and gray below the cliffs. The groomsmen are in uniform, and we bridesmaids wear long dresses of deep-green velvet and carry bouquets of yellow and white mums. The reception follows in the officers' club.

No one asks me to dance during the party. I don't wonder why. I feel awkward and unattractive, so why wouldn't I be left alone? Instead of dancing, I hover in a space near my parents. I don't belong at parties. I don't even belong with people.

"I'm a gargoyle," I tell my parents from the back seat of the car on our way home. My eyes tear up as I say it, but the cruelty of the word feels good to me. I want to hurt all three of us.

"No, you're not," my mother answers quickly.

My father says nothing, and it wouldn't occur to me that the road ahead might swim in his vision, too.

Antigonish (or) The Little Man Who Wasn't There

Yesterday, upon the stair,
I met a man who wasn't there!
He wasn't there again today.
Oh how I wish he'd go away!

When I came home last night at three,
The man was waiting there for me
But when I looked around the hall,
I couldn't see him there at all!
Go away, go away, don't you come back any more!
Go away, go away, and please don't slam the door...

Last night I saw upon the stair,
A little man who wasn't there,
He wasn't there again today
Oh, how I wish he'd go away...   (1899)

(William) Hughes Mearns wrote that poem in 1899. It was part of a play he wrote for a Harvard English class. Mearns called his play, about a haunting in Nova Scotia, *The Psychoed*. The title "Antigonish" is the name of the town where the haunting took place. But the poem's other title, "The Little Man Who Wasn't There," is what interests me. It's a perfect expression of the disconnect between self and material reality when free-floating anxiety hits.

Remember Rollo May?

> *Anxiety (loneliness or "abandonment anxiety" being its most painful form) overcomes the person to the extent that he [sic] loses orientation in the objective world. To lose the world is to lose one's self, and vice versa; self and world are correlates.*

The self is terrified. The encircling world is calm and commonplace. This disjunction feels like madness, which is what I called it when I showed up at a psychiatrist's office the first time.

"What would going crazy be?" he asked.

"Falling to the floor screaming and never being able to stop," I said.

A year after I'd last seen C, the lid came off the chaos in my head. The night that happened, I stared at the pitch-black river from my parents' back porch and wondered how long I could hang on in the terror I was feeling... or if I even wanted to.

Hughes Mearns lived in Edgewater in 1936, but that's just a coincidence.

Grass

By 1967, marijuana was smoked everywhere I went, but I had always turned it down. Maybe I sensed something in myself. But finally, inevitably, I tried it. First time, nothing. Second time, hilarity. Third time, freak-out. Holy Hell, what a night! My mind was all turbulence, and I could sense no ground under me and no horizon to orient myself by. That's how it feels when the world is fine but you are terrified.

The friends I'd smoked with left, my fright ballooned, and finally I had to tell my mother what was going on. Then I asked her to call the cops (*Control! Now! Please!*) because I was clearly going crazy and I was afraid I'd hurt myself. I wanted someone to take control of things. She said absolutely not, no cops, we were not going to do that. She said the two of us would get through the night.

And a hard night it was. One minute, I felt hot and flushed and my heart beat hard and fast in my ears. The next minute, I had chills. Paired muscles on each side of my body clenched and shook. And when I looked down, the muscles were *blue*. I could see the cold in them. My calves clenched and shook. Then my thighs. Then my arms. I shook so hard that my mother had to hold the cup when she fed me warm water. (*"No, not tea. Caffeine will make me shake more."*) And I couldn't stop walking—living room, dining room, kitchen, back porch, kitchen again, hall, living room again. I could see lights in Claire's house from our back porch. (*I wish I were you. I wish I were you.*) My mind thrashed around as if there were two of it wrestling each other. When I could stand still for a moment, my mother held me against her body. I was 21 years old and still a child, living at home and cared for by my mother. I would be here forever; I would never be strong enough to leave. Hours passed and I shook and I paced and I hung on. At dawn I fell asleep.

* * *

When I woke up a couple of hours later, I was nervous and I startled easily, but at least I wasn't terrified and shaking. My vision was blurry, my walk uncoordinated, and I was dog-tired, like after the flu. But I had not dissolved and disappeared; I had wrestled the chaos back down. For the next three hard-swallowing months, I lived at home and went to my classes at Barnard.

"Where is a home? Where is a home for my mind?" I wrote in my journal. "I have no control over it, and the hurtling will begin again sometime."

I swore off grass, of course, but one night, the little man who wasn't there returned. I was studying for a final exam in Japanese when the fright overwhelmed me. I couldn't keep studying. Instead, I pawed through my bookshelves looking for something so bland that I could tether my churning mind to it. I got through to dawn by slowly reading *Kids Say the Darnedest Things*, pure pabulum to focus on, material guaranteed not to fan the terror that had suddenly returned. Once it was light, I woke up my mother. "I'm sick. I need a doctor," I said.

* * *

And I got a doctor, the man who would be my shrink on and off for the next six years, but three weeks after I met him, I was scheduled to go on a summer study program to Japan. He made it clear that I had to make the call myself. My idea of strength is to keep saying "yes" until I can't any longer, so I went. My suitcase held eight weeks of Thorazine tablets. At least I think they were Thorazine, even though I wasn't schizophrenic, just paralyzed by anxiety. The array of psycho-pharmaceuticals was limited in 1967. I did what I could; I lasted two weeks in Japan until I couldn't say "yes" anymore. It was rainy season and I recall no sunshine, just wet darkness. A few things got through my mental morass. I remember the tiny statue of Buddha I saw when I'd climbed up through the Great Buddha statue at Nara. The small statue faced me from inside the Great Buddha's forehead. I felt some peace in it. And I remember a funny moment when our group of young Westerners asked about the soup we'd been served at a ryokan in the countryside. We loved it. The answer came after a consultation with the chef: Campbell's Cream of Potato. A good joke on us. But mostly I remember the rain and dark and anxiety and the feeling that I was floating alone in deep space. I quit the seminar and headed home. Once in Los Angeles, I called my mother every 15 minutes while I waited for a flight back to JFK. All I wanted was to get back to her. That's rock bottom for a 21-year-old. That fall, I dropped out of Barnard.

Sometimes I Get Stuck...

"What did you think ... just then?"
"I saw ... nothing . . . my life."
And then I am sobbing.
"They sound like muffled screams of rage."
"Rage?
"For what?
"No, I'm sad."
I look up.
He raises one eyebrow.
It sounds off to me, too,
not a lie ...
but not a truth.
I don't know my truth.
I never do.
Some truths need capping.
They need controlling.
But all the same,
I take a deep breath to relax
and find a balance point
from which I might
tell the truth.
"I don't want to be mad.
"OK, maybe I am mad ... I know that
"... I know I'm mad ... and
... goddamn it, I know that."

That's as far as I will go.

"I can't find my way today … "

We sit out the rest of my session in silence.

Pacing the Streets

For me, the streets of Edgewater were like the rooms of my own house. I knew all the people I passed on them. The people and things I saw were as familiar as my mom and dad or the photo that had been on their bureau since forever or the slipcover on the couch in our living room. Some people took to pacing those streets when "things got to be too much," a phrase my mother and her friends never explained when I was listening to them. Edgewater streets were safe for those people, like the rooms of their houses, too. As they passed silently by, local people kept an eye on them. When they stalled dumbstruck or in tears in a store or on a corner, someone got them safely home.

Most of those pacers were women. Their troubles wouldn't yield to an afternoon in a bar even if they could bring themselves to go into one alone. Some walked in confusion; some walked so as not to jump out of their own skins; some walked to outdistance their inner pain. Whether confused, agitated, or in pain, each was a closed universe; whatever dilemma lay within remained intensely private as each walked the public streets.

One matron paced town naked under her sheared beaver coat. Perfect circles of bright rouge on her cheeks made her look like a doll. Another woman, a young one, was "Singin' Sam," a nickname the kids gave her. A short and stocky brunette, she walked crooning to a photo of a movie star, maybe Tab Hunter or Rock Hudson. Singin' Sam, we were told, had "been smart" but "thought too much." The grownups said she had "studied too hard," and that was why she had "cracked." Sometimes a grownup told me that I thought too much. *How is that possible?* I'd wonder. I entertained myself puzzling about what I saw: How did the river look when Indians lived here? Did my cats understand what I said? What gave fresh air its smell? Even everyday puzzles like spelling tests or long division problems were fun. I was an only child and had to keep myself company. How could I possibly think too much?

In fact, it was the grownups' language that was imprecise, not their sense of me. What they meant was that I was too sensitive. I got hurt too easily. I spooked too easily. Thinking and feeling both went on in the head, so they'd just say, "You think too much."

That third time I got stoned, I *felt* too much and I felt it *too fast*. My defenses collapsed, and I met my fear suddenly. I tried to get out in front of the pain that followed that collapse, and I too paced the streets of town, mostly at night. Staying in motion helped me with the fear. The walks were bleak. The richness of stories had faded, the river had darkened, and the lines of cliffs, shore, river, and city no longer invited new words. They felt instead like the bars of a cage I was pacing.

Punctuated Disequilibrium

my self is an object I don't feel * the world alarms * images rise and scatter * long months * I compulsively read signs backwards as life jerks and tilts : POTS / SAG / DLEIY / 5 ETUOR / LETOM / 55 TIMIL DEEPS / YAW ENO / LLOT / ADOS / SETTERAGIC / ENOZ LOOHCS * things I settle on that make as much sense as anything else * green pills rattle in the suitcase when I step off into the void * a speedometer hits 100 mph on the Interstate Parkway * Linda chases me with a mascara wand to paint me back to normal * maple walnut ice cream I can't control * my face scares my best friend * a dead boy I barely knew fills my thoughts over and over and over * I put a match flame to my index finger for a focus to stop at * "I'm not sure I want to live" and the little cousin can hear me from the back seat and I don't care * a stick of yellow-green sugar cane on the Staten Island Ferry and somewhere on the ride I let go of showing up for classes * the pills look like Peanut M&Ms and constipate me * I should not be watching *Persona* now * ... so many days ... what did I do besides hang on?

PART THREE
DOWNSTREAM

Dreams to Parse

Telling a psychiatrist my dreams is like being in a *New Yorker* cartoon, especially when he tells me to lie down on the couch, which mine does sometimes. He is in his chair somewhere behind me. We can't look at each other, he says. He says it works better that way when my thoughts are blocked. Sometimes this is okay with me. Sometimes it feels ridiculous. And when it does, I absolutely have to sit up on the edge of the green leather couch to see this man who might be able to help me save my life. If we can't dismantle this anxiety that goes everywhere with me, I might not be able to hold out against it. I don't want to die, but it's so hard to hold up under the fright I feel.

We discuss every detail of my life, no matter how private. That frankness feels wrong at first, like a betrayal of everyone I talk about with him. And I'm reluctant to face whatever ugliness I've hidden under the rocks. But eventually this deeply personal and oddly anonymous conversation feels like the only stable place in my world. We tease meaning out of the day-to-day stories I tell him. What we do feels like a magic wand of words waved at my pain. I have no idea why it works. But, hey presto, it gradually does. An inner certainty rings like a bell whenever we find the truth of what I'm feeling. My dreams, when I'm given them, are like poems that we analyze together to find out who I really am. Like poems, they don't report fact; instead, they report what I feel most deeply. Dreams bring the relief of insight when I wake up in tears or aroused or trying to scream. The best ones—the ones that bring me closest to feeling a coherent self—are horrific or saturated with grief or set in a profound loneliness. They are most-welcome gifts, and I learn to own them.

These are the best dreams I bring to my shrink:

Take Care of Me / Care for Me Dream

It's never lighter than twilight in dreams with my father. They take place in dark brown buildings set in dark brown landscapes; everything is the color of his old corduroy coat. The buildings, whatever they are, overlook the Hudson River from the cliffs or are set on its shore. In this dream, the building is a big old clapboard mansion on River Road where it begins its uphill way to Fort Lee. Some men are chasing me, and I run into the mansion to hide. I'm terrified. If they catch me, they will kill me. I run frantically through empty rooms; the men relentlessly follow. They get closer and closer. Suddenly I have run out of the building, and my father is standing on its lawn near me. "Take care of me, Daddy. Take care of me, Daddy," I wail over and over as I run toward him. As I repeat the words, they change. "Care for me, Daddy. Care for me, Daddy." I wake up from the dream crying.

Corpse Dream

My father and I are standing in the old 125th Street ferry house on the shore of the river. It's night. I sense a growing menace as my father raises his arms to the sky. He circles his arms Prospero-like, and a storm begins to build. Wind rushes. Lightning flashes. Thunder cracks. And with horror, I realize the magic he's up to. He is raising my corpse from the bottom of the river. I plead with him to stop. I cannot survive the sight of my rotting self. I wake up from this dream panting and trying to scream.

Breast Dream

Again my father and I are in growing darkness. He is touching the nipple of my left breast. Primal parts of me beyond words cringe and tense because this is so absolutely wrong. I am powerless to stop it. All I can do is whimper, and I wake up from this dream still whimpering.

Recurring Dream

My father and I live alone in our house. My mother has left, and I am bereft. She has not explained why she left, and she will not tell us where she is. She lives alone somewhere in an apartment like the one we had when I was a child. She sees other people but will not see us. Sometimes I manage to find her apartment, but she's never home when I do. The strangers who answer the door are part of her life, but I am not. Her abandonment of me is a mystery, and it guts me with grief throughout any day that follows this dream.

My shrink says that an adolescent girl especially needs two things from her father as she moves into womanhood: the knowledge that he finds her lovely and the knowledge that she is perfectly safe with him.

"The fact is that you will never be 14 again and close to your father," he adds. "So, where do you go from here?"

Belly Laughs

It took nine months after I first freaked out for me to laugh again, not a long time really. But for every one of those 396,000—give or take—minutes, I walked a precipice. Would I fall over? If I did fall, how far would it be? An infinite distance because I knew I would no longer be me when I hit the bottom. I would likely be nothing. My friends continued their lives at college, but my future had aborted. I hung on at home through gusts of anxiety.

Every Tuesday and Thursday, I went to see my shrink. How could talking to him change the fright I felt? But he was the alternative to giving up. Once, I asked him to commit me, but he said no. Some years later, I asked him why he had refused, and he said he had gambled on the strength he saw in me. He was the only one who saw that strength; maybe that's why I showed up twice a week every week, no matter what. He seemed to assume we were going somewhere. Initially, I just showed up.

But in December, after six months of meeting with him, I laughed again. Just a silly joke with my cousin, but I laughed. Then I laughed even harder describing the joke to a friend. Laughing really hard is a wonderful loss of control, and I laughed so hard tears ran down my face. I laughed so hard, I choked. And none of me disappeared.

Somehow, my shrink and I, rummaging around in the dark bottom of my mind and questioning the things we found there, had turned up enough clues to tease apart my fear. The fear was not a thunderbolt of craziness that had hit me out of nowhere. It was subject to cause and effect. In 1917, a little girl lost her mother and life got scary. The pain of that loss lived on for her. In her loneliness and longing, my mother, that little girl, dreamed of a mother and child so intertwined that no boundary separated them. She would join with her child as she longed to be joined with her lost mother. My childhood had been passed in both her fear and her longing. Sitting on my mother's lap, I'd felt grief like an orphan. The remedy for that was to never split into separate selves. My father, capable and curious, might have cajoled me out into the world, but the unpredictable comings and goings of his drinking and silence undermined my trust in him.

This was not a good recipe for young adulthood, when the world begins to open and it's time to take a chance on yourself and sometimes lose but still grow from it. I had been encouraged to stay safe at home and I hadn't done that. First, I took a chance on a boy. He left and I felt worthless. I took a chance on leaving home for college in Elmira but quit, then took jobs when I was living at home but quit them, then quit Barnard, too, and felt a failure. Then I took a chance on grass and couldn't handle it. Getting hurt, losing my way, getting stoned and freaking out messed with my defenses. The defenses may have been wrong-headed and ripe for removal, but they collapsed too quickly. I didn't grow; I crashed and burned instead. I was lucky and help was nearby. I was desperate and took that help. Eventually, it worked.

And on one wonderful night in New York City, after not so much as a heh-heh since March, I found my laughter again. I was driving on a cross street on the Upper West Side, and my cousin was riding shotgun. The river and the lights of New Jersey were in view ahead. At the curb on my cousin's side, a man exited his parked car. He reached back into the car with his right arm to get something, and his left arm extended behind him into the street. In his left hand was a big holiday gift box, beautifully wrapped in bright red and covered with gold stars that glittered under the streetlight. A big gold bow, perfectly tied, topped it off.

"I'll grab the present then you accelerate," my cousin said out of nowhere. "He won't know what hit him."

And suddenly I was laughing. Why was this so funny? I think because it tapped into some old silliness. On summer nights as children my cousin and I shared a bed in her parents' small apartment at the Jersey shore. Sleepless in the heat, one child would say something silly. The other child would repeat it. Our giggles and snorts would get louder with every repetition. From the living room, the adults would warn us to be quiet. The anticipation of a grownup silhouette backlit in the bedroom door would ratchet up our tension and result in louder laughter. One or two more warnings would be called out from the living room before that looming silhouette arrived to deliver the "last warning." We didn't hear it because we were by then heaving and shaking with stifled laughter and were going to explode if the grownup didn't leave soon. When the door finally closed, we laughed so hard into our pillows that we drooled and shed tears.

My laughter that night on the West Side was my testimony to the pure fun of being alive and behaving badly with a co-conspirator, just like when we were seven years old at the shore. The interplay between the perfectly wrapped gift, the unknowing victim, and we two desperados was hilarious. Something let go of me a little, and life started to look again like work I could do.

Dust

The store on Ninth Avenue
Sold fabric.
Hundreds of bolts were
Stacked on shelves and stood on end
And set here and there
Across the old wood counters.
So much fabric that

My eyes and nose stung
From the chemicals that sized it.
We came for fabric,
My mother and I.
We came looking for fabric
To make me a dress
And for a zipper that matched
Or maybe buttons in the same shade.
Waiting for the thump
Of the next thick bolt tossed on the counter,
I looked toward the street
For no reason except I was bored.
Rays of late-day sun slanted
Through the old display windows
And specks of dust danced in that light.
Customers leaned over the counters
To study bolts of fabric.
I watched the dust specks spin
In the waterfall of weightless light.
The dust. The golden light. And me.
And I remembered:
My home, I'm home.

My Stupendously Lucky Life-Altering Random Encounter

I still lived at home with my parents, but I didn't feel stranded there anymore. I was working at a small newspaper in Hudson County. Before that newspaper job, my prospects for earning money were dim. I'd already failed to get jobs at a foam-rubber factory and in the typing pool at a publishing house. The factory boss talked to me for two minutes then said I had too much education. Just as well because my father had drawn a line in the sand and said that I couldn't live in his house if I took that job. At the publishing house, I passed the typing test, but the office manager said "no, thanks" when she found out I typed with two fingers.

Then along came a newspaper job and the whole rest of my life. I found it through someone I met as I carried a Eugene McCarthy petition around Edgewater. He couldn't sign the petition, but he gave me a ticket into newspapers instead. On newspapers, they didn't care how many fingers you typed with. This was pre-Watergate, before half the kids in the country wanted to be reporters. At this point, reporting was a gray-collar job; you didn't need a degree to get in the door and you could type with your nose as long as you met deadline.

"Can you write?" my fairy godfather asked me when I told him I was looking for a job.

"I don't know. I like to. I got A's on school papers," I said.

He considered the two North Jersey newspapers where he'd worked and where hiring editors would take his calls. He decided to send me to the smaller one, the *Hudson Dispatch*; it was an easier bar for me to clear with no experience.

"That way, you'll have time to learn," he said.

While I sat there, he called the managing editor. It was a Sunday night. By Monday afternoon, I'd been interviewed and hired. By Tuesday afternoon, I was taking notes from the police log in Ridgefield Park. It wasn't "my" town; I didn't have my own town yet. I was the sub on the regulars' nights off. But even though I was second string, cops and mayors and borough clerks took my calls and answered my questions. I had a pass on my car visor that said PRESS. It wasn't as iconic as one tucked into the band of a 1940s fedora, but it made a standout statement on my parents' street in Edgewater. And it got me past police lines in Bergen County. Hudson County was a tougher audience, and, for the next six months until I quit that paper, the street kids around my office in Union City would yell "Press what?" every single time they saw me pull up. Every. Single. Time.

As it turned out, after some instruction, I *could* write up a respectable mayor and council meeting or zoning board hearing. Town government, non-existent to me a month before, became my everyday. I was *never* bored in the city room. It was a brightly lit, 24/7 story factory filled with the noise of telephones, wire machines, and people pounding big black typewriters. There was always someone to talk to and something to talk about.

One Monday night featured a delegation of Hudson County Black Panthers who arrived to point out some problems in our coverage of the group. The six Panthers crowded into the managing editor's office. This white-haired man wore a wide tie, a starched shirt, and, yes, sleeve garters. The Panthers did not look friendly. Little by little everyone in the city room stopped typing and stared at the glass wall of the ME's tiny office. Behind the glass, arms waved and voices got loud. But after 20 minutes, the negotiations unexpectedly ended with handshakes. The Panthers seemed satisfied and left. Relief flooded the city room; the paper had no security staff.

The whole country was seething in the spring of 1968. Twice the bells on the AP and UPI wire machines rang rare high alerts. The first time, the wires announced the murder of Martin Luther King Jr. in Memphis. The second time was for the murder of Robert F. Kennedy in Los Angeles. On those nights, reporters stayed late to gather reaction from their towns. When we finally finished the phone calls after the King killing and left work, the patrons of our usual bar in Union City were celebrating King's death. We moved on to Clahan's, a bar in Edgewater, where we could share our shock and sadness with just the bartender looking on. We never went back to that bar in Union City. Clahan's became our place to decompress after the midnight deadline. It was down among the factories in Shadyside, and by the time we would show up, the shift workers were long gone and the bar was empty.

The events we covered for this small newspaper shifted giddily from tragedy to comedy. We wrote about the murders of King and Kennedy, but on full moon nights, the Fairview Bra and Girdle Thief would strike. We'd write up the police report that was in the duty log the next day: Ladies' undergarments had been stolen yet again from clotheslines in Fairview backyards. The working theory in the police station was that it was the full moon that made this guy restless every month. The cops assumed it was a guy. Men's underwear was left untouched on the lines.

The city room staff itself was a cast of characters. My favorite was a gray-haired copy editor who had worked at the *Straits Times* in Singapore. He wore a white flannel suit and a straw fedora to work all summer. He was unfailingly polite, a soft-spoken alcoholic who lived in a rented room in Jersey City. Copy editors often worked their whole careers at night. Some became alcoholics and almost all had complicated or lonely personal lives, a chicken-or-the-egg kind of problem. But it didn't affect their editing. In those linotype days, the copy editors were "last before lead" and they took the role seriously, even after drinking their suppers. I never had cause to complain about any edits they made in my stories.

The clerk who delivered reporters' stories and copy from the wires to editors was a very short, round, cranky man. His bad humor was understandable; he shed patches of skin, and the psoriasis left raw, red areas behind that must have been painful. He wore a yellowing dress shirt every night, always pressed, and brown trousers held up by suspenders. He limped slowly around the city room scowling, and we were careful not to get stuck in a corner behind him as he passed. Only a few old ceiling fans stirred the air, and they were not enough to blow away the smell of dead skin.

My work nights were lively and defied prediction. One night I'd be on assignment at a dock fire where flames shot up 80 feet over the Hudson River. The next night I'd be in an embalming room interviewing the owner of a new funeral parlor. (Funeral directors placed death notices, and death notices brought advertising dollars to a small paper, so our small paper published features about new funeral homes.) Sometimes cops flirted with me when I picked up news at police stations. One grabbed a bag of marijuana from an evidence box and tossed it at me. "Know what that is?" We played catch with it for a while.

My father liked this job for me and was happy that the prospect of work at a foam rubber factory had faded. His threat to throw me out disappeared. I doubt he would have done it. Love would have trumped control for him. I stayed on in our house paying minimal room and board. That was crucial because ever since I'd taken the job, I'd been saving money for a trip to Europe, a plan floated by a friend from the first college I quit, Carolyn Carr. My personal deadline at the paper—July 31—was set before I even started, but I hadn't told my bosses. When the time came to quit, I'd lie and tell them that another friend of Carolyn's had bailed on the trip and offered me her plane ticket. Newspapers would shape my whole adult life, but at this point, I was there to finance an adventure.

Anxiety still struck sometimes, but I'd gotten some ground under my feet. The attacks were fewer and I could power through them. Carolyn's plan to hitchhike around Europe until her money ran out sounded like a great next step, and I said yes to her.

An Alphabet of Guys

D Is for Doppleganger
(Soundtrack: *Suzanne* by Leonard Cohen)

After two years of celibacy, I find a C lookalike at work: thin and tall, blond hair, blue eyes, glasses, but instead of a cupid's bow, his lips are a straight line. Severe, not naughty. Oh well. The thrill here, for both of us but for different reasons, is that I'm not committed. In six months more or less, I'll be hitchhiking around Europe with Carolyn, and my ticket home will have an open return date. D knows this from the beginning. I feel a heady sense of freedom, and D is attracted to that. He's cheating on his longtime girlfriend, feeling guilty, and writing me love poems about it. We work nights together at the newspaper and finish at midnight. Usually we have a drink with the other reporters before we go to his apartment for sex. I'm amazed by how much easier sex is when I feel I have nothing to lose. He's even competitive about it. "I will not be out-fucked," D tells me in bed one night when my knees are somewhere up near my ears. Sometimes, before we get to his apartment, we park and make out. One night, our steamed-up windows attract a cop. "Get a room," he tells us when we answer his tap on the roof. In fact, we have D's whole apartment somewhere in Belleville. But our frame of mind is immediate, and that's the kind of relationship we have. I don't much care about cops now. Promiscuity, it turns out, is easy. It's intimacy that's hard.

   Most nights, it's still dark when I leave D and drive home to my parents' house. I sleep until noon and start work again at 3. I'm 22 years old and it's a sweet deal. The days pass quickly, and I don't worry about love or work. An old boyfriend comes back into my life. A cop asks me out. After a while, I'm seeing three guys at once and lying to all of them. I have absolutely nothing to lose, so I'm having fun. But playing the field and keeping my stories straight gets hectic. It's a relief when our Icelandic Airlines flight to Luxembourg taxis down a runway at JFK and I leave them all behind. I officially end things only with D. For the next three or four months, my mother nervously juggles visits by the other two guys. At least the visits were a distraction from her fears for me on the road in Europe. I didn't realize how deeply worried she'd been until the afternoon three months later when I was home again. She'd disappeared after I gave out gifts I'd bought and told a few Europe stories. I found her in a back bedroom sobbing with relief.

On the Road

Photo by Carolyn S. Carr

The Leif Eiriksson

I can't remember if our flight to Europe took off in the day or night, but I *can* clearly remember my first sight of the plane. If you are young in 1968, you fly on Loftleidir, Iceland's airline. It has the cheapest fares and lands you in Luxembourg in the heart of Western Europe, where you can activate a Eurail Pass and take the next train to wherever appeals to you next. Our plane out of JFK is the *Leif Eiriksson*. The name is written on its side in bright blue cursive. The Rolls Royce logos on its shiny engines reassure me about our no-frills, prop-plane flight over the Atlantic. But Leif the Lucky, the Viking seafarer, is my true lodestar. Finally, I'm headed out and away from home and childhood. I have my open airplane ticket, my Eurail pass, and $520 in travelers' checks. I am barely ready for this adventure, but barely ready would be enough. I learn that over and over.

Luxembourg, astoundingly, is there to meet us. Images of Europe from magazines and postcards stand life size all around me. The Old World of cobblestone streets, needle-thin spires, and stucco and stone buildings looks like the set of a WWII movie. Speaking French or German, people hurry past on what sounds like interesting and urgent business. I feel alive and ready to meet them. My trip to Japan was a dark dream. I was sick with anxiety and dulled by Thorazine, and I crawled through two weeks of it before I gave up. But on the bus in from the Luxembourg airport, I am as excited as I am exhausted. I'm restarting my conversation with the world. A quote from my journal midflight over the Atlantic reads: "8/8/68 somewhere over the Atlantic Ocean, we lost a day and gained a whole new world ... a year ago I wanted to die."

In the months ahead, all the world's young people seem to be on the move with us. It's 1968, and everywhere we go the cars, trucks, buses, third-class train compartments, and cheap airlines of Europe and the UK are filled with people our age. We form a floating community that chatters in polyglot conversations and trades advice on how to keep our trips going as long as possible. Just a glance or smile at a stranger can open hours of talk, shared meals, even days traveling together. We make a whole world for ourselves.

At the youth hostel, I put 100 Luxembourg francs (about $2) on the counter with my American Youth Hostel card, and Carolyn does the same. That gets each of us a sleeping bag for a night, a dormitory bed, a cold shower, and breakfast. The young man at the counter leads us upstairs, where we pass through two shower rooms to get to the door of our dormitory. It holds 12 clean bunks, all but two occupied. Among the 10 other women is a French woman in her early

20s like us. Her name is Jouraud. I have some French; she has some English. The three of us talk and I translate until, exhausted, we all have to sleep.

The next morning, Carolyn and I are standing in front of the hostel trying to figure out where to get a bus to the train station when a tiny purple Renault rolls up and stops. A window rolls down, and Jouraud hangs out.

"Hey, Americans, are you still planning to go to Amsterdam?" she calls out. We nod. "Get in. My brother and our friend are driving to Eindhoven after they drop me at the airport. Two open seats in the car! You can get a train to Amsterdam from Eindhoven."

Carolyn and I look at each other to gauge our reactions to a ride with complete strangers. Is this in any way wise? I have the false courage of a teargas pen in my pocket for emergencies, and we are already pumped on adventure. Of course we get in. I never need that pen in Europe. In fact, having it comes to feel ridiculous. Most people not only give us rides but also buy us tea or coffee and feed us. And that's exactly what our new friends, Jean Louis and Louis, do—coffee at the frontier between Luxembourg and Belgium and a hearty lunch at Louis's house in Eindhoven. His parents don't seem to find it odd that the world-traveling son they haven't seen for several years has shown up with a Frenchman he's known for four days and two Americans he met that morning. They lay out a meal of bread and butter, cheese, eggs, and coffee and urge us to eat up. European hospitality will pack pounds on me over the months that follow.

* * *

The experiences that pile up as we wander around Europe for three months are mine in a way experiences have not been since childhood. I don't watch myself do things. I lead my life and feel it for the most part without filters, barriers, or distance, and it stuffs my head with riches. I keep journals. Carolyn is learning photography and takes pictures. We take small risks and some that are too large. We are open with strangers and flirt with young men. We master new cities, sometimes in spite of languages neither of us understand. We get sick and we get better. We are cheated in Dublin and groped in Florence and love both cities anyway. We arrive in Portugal right after Salazar has a cerebral hemorrhage and stay in a tense garrison town, but what I remember is eating pomegranates off the trees on our way to the beach. We are rescued off a slope in Lugano after running through a railway tunnel we never should have been in. We pick grapes on a French farm and live in a cowshed there. We are flaneurs before I ever hear the word. We have a great time.

* * *

From My Journals

Amsterdam: "Today we gave a 2 guilder tip to a guide for a 2½ guilder boat ride—I thought he'd fall overboard—dumb, dumb, dumb move." … "645 bridges, 60 miles of canals, 30,000 ships a year, 600,000 bicycles, 900,000 inhabitants" … "I can't figure Dutch out at all. My ordering in a restaurant today produced a raw meat sandwich." … "I felt a terrible claustrophobia in Anne Frank's hiding place." … "An Algerian teacher we met on the street rolled a cigarette for Carolyn that looked like she was smoking a roll of paper towels." … "Amsterdam is a young city, streets full of young people, and when you sit in Dam Square on the monument steps, no one asks you to move on."

Copenhagen: "Even youth hostel rooms were in short supply, so I called my aunt's friend Celestin Pouliot, a Catholic brother who works for the Papal Nuncio. It took me 45 minutes to master the Danish phone protocol. Cel told me to call back in an hour. When I did, we were on. He put us up for free in the attic rooms of the Bishop of Copenhagen's house. The bishop is away on a trip." …

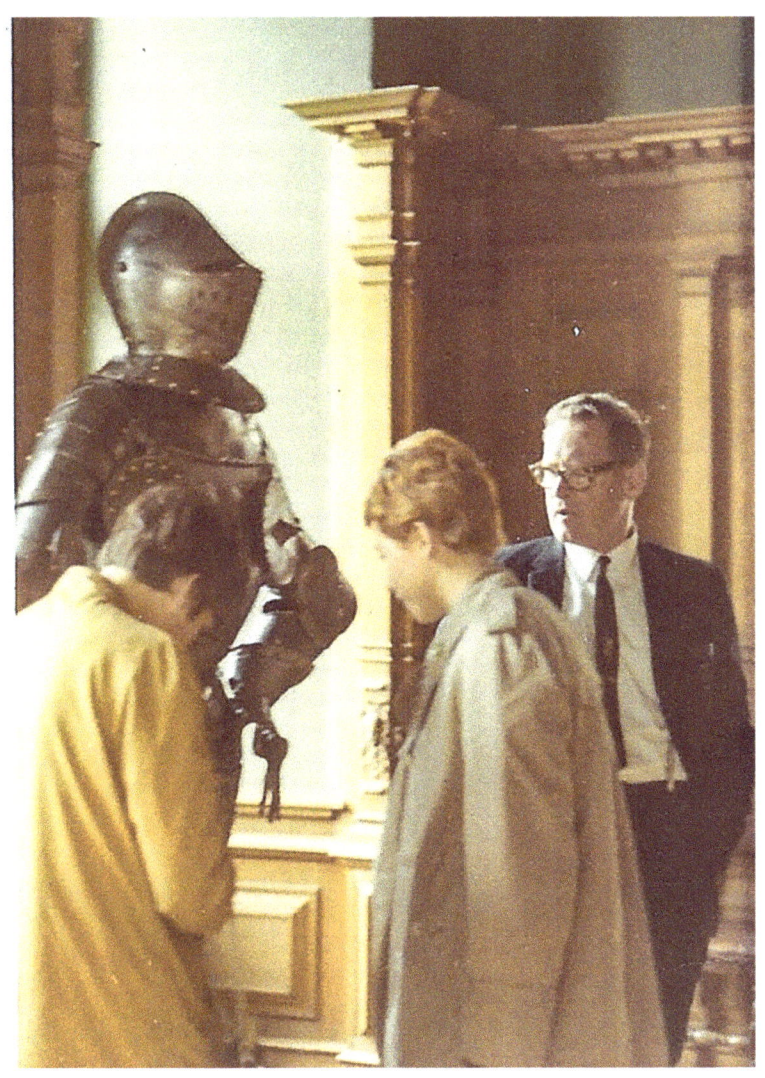

Sightseeing with Brother Cel

Photo by Carolyn S. Carr

"The smell of the sea is everywhere on the wind." ... "The Danes say, 'There is no bad weather, only different kinds.' They picnic even in the snow." ... "The nun who keeps house here invited us for breakfast where we met the finance officer for the Diocese of Copenhagen. He said Danes back [Eugene] McCarthy and prefer the Democrats but dislike Humphrey because he's 'all politics and politics are generally dirty.' "

Vedbaek: "The bishop is returning, so Cel moved us north to a big, weirdly empty mansion the Church owns near the sea on a road called Caroline Mathildevej. I took a picture of Carolyn under her street sign." ... "Perhaps there is no bad weather, but with a tight head and chest cold, there is no good weather either." ... "We rode bikes down to the beach and stopped at a *polser* wagon for supper. *Polser* are long hot dogs on hot rolls and covered with ketchup, mustard, sweet and sour sauce, raw onions and fried onions. Mmmmm." ... "People are open and friendly, not tight and closed. I'm relaxed and happy here. I can't say enough about this difference. I can't look at it like I would at a cathedral; I just feel it shine all over me."

Carolyn in Vedbaek

Photo by Author

Train from Oslo to Bergen: "Russia has invaded Czechoslovakia 8/20-21/68."

Spur-of-the-Moment Sidetrip to Flam: "Ears popping and popping through the 12-mile descent from Myrdal on the Bergensbanen to Flam on the Aurlandsfjord. Our carriage was filled with Norwegian men headed home to the valley after work." ... "We went to the general store where we bought a huge piece of goat's milk cheese and some apples for breakfast. We walked a ways along the road to Arundel then climbed up the rock at a nice place and sat down to eat in a hollow lined with moss, grass, and some lavender flowers. Later we walked through a farm where they raise ermine or maybe they were white mink. They must have had 500 of them in cages, and when we came near, they ran in circles like poor crazy things. If you looked only at their cute faces, you could ignore the fact that they look an awful lot like rats."

Workers going home on Flam railway

Photo by Carolyn S. Carr

Bergen: "The harbor is surrounded by hills so I can see the water, the fish market, and the boat and ship traffic from our room." ... "I feel at home. A lot of the older women look just like Mom." ... "The merchants' houses from the days of the Hanseatic League have cupboard beds like in a ship. I'd love to have a bed like that." ... "My mother's cousin Anna took us to see the house where my grandfather was born; it's tiny and made of yellow clapboard." ... "The cousins—Anna; her husband, Halfdan; her daughter, Randi; her brother, Haakon (who looks just like Grandpa); and Haakon's wife, Borne, took us on the funicular up Mount Floyen, where we danced and ate and drank until midnight as fog filled the city below. Haakon danced the legs off me and Carolyn, but they were impressed that I could keep up with them eating." ...

Randi, Anna, and I on Mount Ulriken

Author's Photo

"At *Skipshuset*, a museum of excavated objects ca. 1000 AD to 1500 AD in the old town, I found my trip keepsake, a gold copy of a signet ring from the excavations and dating from the 1200s." … "The smell of herring is everywhere we go." … "Anna told me my grandfather was a 'real ladies man,' who in addition to being married three times in the States, 'left many ladies in Bergen with tears in their eyes.' " … "Goat cheese, caraway cheese, and old cheese, all Norwegian everyday fare, are by far the weirdest and best we've had on our trip." … "We had supper at Anna's and dessert at Haakon's. Haakon's son, Rune, had brought his friend Ariel. It's the damndest thing to hear him play guitar and sing a perfectly accented Roger Miller or Hank Williams song then suddenly talk to Rune in Norwegian. He memorized the songs accent and all!" … "Anna is worried for the Czechs. She says, 'We Norwegians know what it is like to be occupied; so quickly it happens and we were so shocked and so confused. We understand how those people feel.' " … "Anna bought and shipped big hunks of goat cheese to the States for us. She and Randi saw us off on the night boat to Newcastle."

Night Boat to Newscastle: "The third person in our cabin was Mrs. Reggie Hepworth, who told us, 'Oh, I know the war was grim and all that, but I had a perfectly lovely time. It was so exciting.' The Hepworths squeezed us into their car, treated us to sandwiches and drinks, and dropped us off at a service stop outside Doncaster, our first leg to London. … One lorry ride took us on past Leicester, and a second truck driver offered us a hitch all the way to London. 'What do you carry?' we asked him. 'Anything,' he laughed. 'I picked you two up, didn't I?' … He was small and tough, tattooed and the nicest kind of tease, and he bought us meat pasties and coffee."

"What do you carry?" we asked him
Photo by Carolyn S. Carr

London: "London is freezing cold, and the chill comes into our hostel room through the old windows. Carolyn pulled apart a plastic shopping bag, peeled tape off the gift wrapping of our purchases, and covered the windows. Still cold!" ... "We walked on Regent Street, on Oxford Street, in Trafalgar Square, in Soho Square, in Piccadilly Circus, in St. John's Wood, in Marylebone, and Hampstead, etc., today. I have huge blisters under my toes from walking all day on the Dr. Scholl's sandals." ... "We began to hear about the Democratic Convention in Chicago. 'It's quite a savage country, isn't it?' a young man said to me." ... "Sightseeing today. We walked along the Thames, saw St. Paul's Cathedral, the Tower of London and the Crown Jewels, Hyde Park, and Speakers' Corner."

Hitch to Liverpool: "Oh Lord another day of such moving about. Thumbs out by 8 am and we got a lift from a hairdresser who left us on an M1 approach road where we were picked up by two diddley-boppers about 18 years old, Stephen and Russ. Their radio was booming and we flew up the M1. Carolyn and I were folded into the back seat of the Triumph. Stephen was headed to a party in Liverpool, where we can get the ferry to Dublin. Carolyn calculated that we saved $35 by hitching everywhere in England."

Dublin: "The first thing that happened to us in Ireland was to be gypped out of a shilling by a cabdriver whose dashboard was loaded with plastic Christs, Madonnas and St. Christophers. We got a double room with breakfast, shared bathroom, and no heat for less than 50 cents a night plus extra for a bath. And what a breakfast! Mrs. Grealey served dark and light bread, butter, marmalade, tea, grapefruit, egg, sausages, bacon, and fried bread. We needed it. We walked around Dublin for 10 hours afterward: St. Michan's Church for the mummies; Dublin Castle; Christ Church Cathedral for evensong service; and the Lantern Theater to see *Molly and Anna*, monologues from *Ulysses* and *Finnegans Wake*. I preferred down-to-earth Molly to witty, fey Anna." ... "No matter how wretched a building is the door is always newly painted, with a sparkling polished brass knob, bell, and mail slot, and there are palm trees all over the city!" ... "On the Guinness Brewery tour, we met a guy from Princeton who turned out to know one of my high school friends. We spent the whole evening pub hopping, but we didn't even trade last names. Everyone is always headed away the next day." ... "We took a bus to Dalkey for Joyce. About ¼ mile out into the water, across a thrashing green sea, lies Dalkey Island, one large lump of land that trails off into a few naked rocks on its northern end. Green grass was spread over the top like a bad toupee. At the southern part of the island, I could see the Martello tower, built of sandy colored rock with one black eye window staring at me across the channel. We weren't able to get a boat to the island because the sea was too rough, so we walked back into town and stopped for an Irish coffee at a pub."

Flight to Paris: "Practicing my French: *Ah, les Francais, la salle de bain ici sur l'aeroplane etait un peu derangee mais il y avait une grande boteille de cologne la pour tous les personnes d'employer.*"

Paris: "Got rooms in the rue de Gay-Lussac in the Grand Hotel du Progres. Bidet in the room but I can't figure it out. Two French doors (what other kind of doors would they be?) leading to our own tiny balcony and a WC down the hall. Out for late supper and Carolyn paid 11 cents or 12 cents per glass for white wine." ... "We used the bidet in our room for a footbath, and it felt great." ... "Even in Paris, the bourgeois in me will out. I did my laundry in the bidet this lovely Monday morning. After wearing the same dress, slip, and bra the whole time in Dublin, I've discovered a strain of dirt that *can* hide from intensified Tide." ... "No sightseeing today, but here's a partial list of places we noodled around: Colonne Vendome, Hotel de Ville, Louvre, Notre Dame, Opera, Palais de Justice, Palais de Luxembourg, Pantheon, Ste. Mary Madeleine, Sorbonne, Tour Eiffel, Sainte Chappelle, Place de la Concorde, les Champs-Elysses, les Tuileries, Pont St. Michel, Pont Neuf, Ile de la Cite, Jardins de Luxembourg, the flower markets, along the Left and Right Banks, the Latin Quarter, St. Germain des Pres, Jeu de Paume, Boul' St. Mich', Rue de Rivoli, Palais Royale, Boulevard de la Madeleine, Boulevard des Capucines, Boulevard des Italiens, les quais, Hotel Dieu. We walked from about 10 am to 10 pm. My blisters now number 10, five per foot. The city is the most beautiful I've ever seen." ... "I visited les Invalides, the damndest biggest-feeling grandest-feeling place I've ever been in." ... "All of Paris, perhaps all of France, takes a two-hour lunch. Carolyn says it's because they have lunch and make love." ... "At a youth group called Concordia, we signed up for three weeks of picking grapes in the Pyrenees in October. The camp will provide room, board, and a little money, so we've extended our time in Europe by three weeks. And, I handled all the arrangements in French!"

Train from Paris to Madrid: "I felt guilty that we were riding in first class, but the atmosphere in second class gets kind of close. I don't mind garlic or wine or people sacked out all over, but I get uptight when I'm gawked at or touched or propositioned in a language I don't understand." ... "A sign in the train washroom read: 'Turn the handle indifferently to obtain water.' "... "A soldier in a patent leather hat and carrying a gun got on at San Sebastian and sat in our compartment. He was carrying eight briefcases that were handcuffed together and to him! I like to think they were filled with secret government documents."

Madrid: "Only expensive singles were left when we got to where the tourist bureau sent us, but the deskman there sent us on to a hostel across the street where we got a double and continental breakfast for 60 pesetas [a little over $1] a night each. It's shabby, but it's relatively clean, cheap and the people are nice." ... "I outfitted myself for the work camp with a sleeping bag, frame backpack, plastic cloth for the ground, dish, canteen, cutlery, plastic glass, and a plastic box for food for about $20. I also got shoes that won't hurt my feet, blue and white striped espadrilles. They look very happy down there at the bottom of my legs." ... "We had our first supper at a tapas *meson*, where we tasted squid, stuffed pimento, huge fried peppers, fried eggplant, eggs stuffed with fish, chunks of bonito in vinegar, tiny snails, bacon rind, fish balls, and artichoke hearts. We stuffed ourselves for about

$1.50 each." ... "Carolyn said I'm more exclusively in my own head than anybody she knows. We had long talks and great ideas tonight but no record of them as this scribe is pooped—*buenos noches*." ... "Bosch's brain is dead and dust more than 400 years, but it spoke to me in the 20th century through symbols for the chaos I felt when I freaked out. At the Prado, we also saw van der Weyden's *Descent from the Cross*, and no matter what a professor shows you in a slide about the work's movement, you'll never know it until you stand before that painting and swivel your head following its lines."

Lisbon then by Boat and Train to Faro: "I am filthier than I've ever been, dirty hair, dirty feet, dirty body, dirty nails and I sit dreaming of Faro waves and sunbeams, of warmth and lots of water, of days spent in one place, no interesting sights, no personally compelling pilgrimages, just rest and contemplation and getting a tan before we trek to the *David*, the Alps, and to get rid of these bloody suitcases before the work camp." ... "A lame woman came around to everyone in the waiting room and begged money then sat down and told a story for about 10 minutes as her way of earning what they gave. I don't know what she said, but she told it with vigor to the whole room and had many attentive listeners." ... "I'm 22 years old. How could I not have known that in Portugal I was on the Atlantic Ocean, not the Mediterranean Sea?"

Faro: "Got a place in a pension where we have a one-bed double and continental breakfast for 69 escudos tonight (just under $2.50) then 61 escudos each successive night, extra for baths." ... "It's strange to me that in Catholic countries the men are the most aggressive we've met. Our new American friend Jerry says it's logical because they're the most frustrated." ... "Carolyn and I have been immediate and direct with our decisions on this trip, but all of a sudden, things got foggy when we arrived in Faro, and we were just pissing around. I realized it's because we're so used to men making decisions that we had deferred to Jerry to get us into town and a pension. And he just stood there. We talked about it later, and he said his father is retiring and mild and his mother is dominant." … "In the back of a poetry book I bought in Dublin was an ad that said, 'Miroslav Holub would like people to read poems as naturally as they read the papers, or go to a football match. Not to consider it as anything more difficult, or effeminate, or praiseworthy.' "… "We saw the skeleton of a lizard caught on the spines of a cactus." … "Feel so good, so curious about the world and all it holds and how I fit in." … "Jerry's been chatting with people who tell him that Salazar is near death after 43 years of ruling with an iron hand, and no successor is apparent. The Portuguese seem to assume that civil war will break out when he dies." … "The enigma of the bidet continues. The water does not shoot up in the air like Aunt Lucy said it did." … "A lame boy about 10 years old begged from me in the evening. Around 1 a.m., Carolyn was already asleep, and I finished reading, turned off the lights, and went to the window for a last look around. He was hobbling across the empty square alone under the street lamp."… "After oversleeping in the heat, I was rushing around in the dark as we packed to leave Faro, and I accidentally killed one of our bathroom roaches. Ai! We'd both been so careful with them."

Between Trains in Lisbon: "No card from Concordia about our work camp, so we'll have to go to their office in the two hours we have between trains in Paris. But there was a lovely letter from my mother. She tried to write in a way that showed her love but still acknowledged my independence from her. She knows I need that balance. No letter from Dad. Mom wrote that he worried I might get homesick reading it, like I did reading the one I got in Japan. This trip is sometimes scary for them."

On the Sud Express, Lisbon to Hendaye: "Carolyn shook me awake to two Spanish officials who had been trying to wake us up for our passports. The men were laughing '*Americanas! Americanas!*' "

Paris: "The news at Concordia was OK. If they don't have enough people for a work camp, we'll work for M. Dumon, the vineyard owner, and be paid a wage as grape pickers, working 10 hours a day. We report to him the evening of 10/11." … "French women and Spanish men are the most appealingly perfumed people in the world. Yum!"

Train to Luxembourg: "When we went for coffee and tea, we struck up a conversation with the conductor and the barman, who gave us huge free glasses of red wine that they called 'French coffee.' They said de Gaulle has done much for *la gloire* of France but zero for *les ouvriers*, and they seemed genuinely sad to hear that in the States we were told the French disliked Americans and treated them coldly."

Barman on train to Luxembourg

Photo by Carolyn S. Carr

Lugano: "All nine youth hostels were full, and the staff at one suggested we get back on a train and go to Como instead. We bagged that idea, bought some crispy autumn apples, dried fruit, and nuts, and sat on a corner in the sun reading the *International Herald Tribune* we bought in Paris and watching Lugano pass by. Then we went to the local *turismo*, which sent us to a dormitory for transients and long-term residents run by Catholic nuns. Hot wash water, too, but you pay extra to take a bath or shower." … "A fellow yodeled at us while we were walking around the lake!" … "I dreamt that a friend from Edgewater described a girl the police were looking for. The dream description reminded me of Sylvia Plath's *Lady Lazarus*: 'red hair, totally freaked out on acid and pills, really insane.' In the exaggerated language of dreams, the description fit me at my worst times." … "We finally have toilet paper in the bathroom here, neatly ripped strips of newspaper. If I don't have printer's ink in my blood, I will have it on my crotch. Carolyn said I'll get a Pubitzer Prize." … "Carolyn and I almost killed ourselves by falling off the bottom of an Alp today. We walked down from the topmost lookout on Monte San Salvatore and had lunch in the restaurant where the funicular stops. After lunch, we headed down the mountain on foot. The walk was beautiful—wooded paths and then meadows covered with thousands of little grasshoppers jumping up as we walked across—and one spot so empty and ours that we danced crazy and rolled around in the fallen leaves. When we got to the shore of the lake, we walked along the highway that rims it. The Sunday traffic was heavy, the Italian drivers were speeding, and there was no sidewalk, so we were all over the place trying to find a safe space to walk in. We climbed onto a wall that separates the highway from the train tracks on the lakeshore. As we walked, the wall got higher, and I got dizzy between the cars passing on the left and the trains passing on the right, so we jumped down from the wall and walked next to the tracks toward Lugano. It was scary then to remember how many times we'd seen men toss empty wine bottles out train windows. Along the way, we ran through a tunnel. That seemed OK because it was short and there was lots of room on each side next to the tracks. We figured that the lake shoreline would lead us back to Lugano, so we kept going. But eventually we found ourselves in a cul de sac—a 30-foot wall up to the highway on our left; a long, dark train tunnel ahead with no side room along the tracks; 300 feet of steep, wooded hillside down to the lake on our right; and behind us, just the nerve-racking way we'd come. After a bit of poking about, we found a narrow path to the right of the tunnel and followed its incline hoping to get to the highway. When the path ended, the slope we'd climbed up was too steep to get back down, so we kept clawing our way through brambles until we reached a little tree 50 feet farther up, and both of us grabbed it. Below us were hundreds of feet to the lake, a potentially lethal fall. Above us were still 20 near-vertical feet to the top of the slope and then a 7-foot stone wall. At first, I didn't want to make a fuss by calling for help, but when I felt the tree's roots begin to rise in the dirt under my feet, I stopped feeling silly and started yelling. A house sat some 200 feet through the woods to our right, and a hefty signora came out when she heard me. She peered through the trees at us then hurried over to a restaurant nearby on the highway. Soon a bunch of gesticulating men ran out of it, swarmed over the wall toward us, and formed a human chain. A meaty hand shot through the brambles in front of my face, grabbed my hand, and I was hauled from one man to the next over the last 20 feet then pushed up and over the wall. Curious customers from the restaurant had filled the parking lot by then. I heard the rescuers call out, '*Un otro, un otro.*' Next Carolyn popped over the wall followed by the men, and we were saved. I was laughing and crying and hugging Carolyn and kissing all the rescuers and repeating '*Grazie. Grazie.*' Two of our rescuers were young Italians who had been at the restaurant. They were 'mods'—long hair, elegant nipped-waist jackets, and bellbottoms. As we walked towards the restaurant, bloodied by scratches, filthy, and a bit hysterical, one of them grabbed my left hand and asked, '*Sposato?*' When I said 'no,' he gave a happy shout. For once, I didn't mind the aggressive flirting—the guy had saved us *and* he was handsome. After we cleaned up in the Ladies, the two young men had glasses of cognac waiting on their table for us. I belted mine and hardly felt it; my hands kept on shaking. Our hosts made good-natured fun of us;

apparently, as we hung from the tree calling for "ropes," I was yelling for 'string' in French and Carolyn was yelling for 'clothes' in Spanish. While we didn't have a firm grip on each others' languages, when our two rescuers called out '*Aiudar! Aiudar!*' in falsetto voices and then struck superhero poses, we all laughed. These lovely guys invited us to go dancing with them when we get to Milano, where they live, but told us to 'wear nice clothes that night.' Then they drove us the five kilometers back to Lugano in a silver Alfa Romeo GTO with its radio blasting *Applausi*. Paolo stopped once to argue with a traffic cop, and when he leapt out of the driver's seat, I had to push the brake with my hand from the passenger side because we were rolling into a busy intersection. The guys laughed when we told them we were staying with nuns. They laughed even harder when they asked for a pen to give us their phone number, and I pulled a stray twig out of my bag. I don't think they understood at all why we had been in that tree, but that's OK because each two of us thought the other two were crazy and fun. Tonight, I emptied smashed elderberries out of my dress pockets when I changed for bed." … "Rented a Pedalo to cruise on the lake today. As we got back to the dock, I recognized a girl from the restaurant where we went after our rescue. I saw her point to the mountain then us and say something to a guy running the Pedalo rental, whose eyes widened. We compounded his impression of us by crashing the Pedalo into the dock." … "I get lazy when I'm sick, so we never made it to Milan. Carolyn wanted to, but we were both getting colds, and I didn't want to make the extra travel plans or buy shoes I could dance in."

Florence: "Some dirty old son-of-a-bitch poked me right in the crotch on our way to the hostel. This is the city of Cellini, Michelangelo, and Leonardo? Ptui!" … "The *turismo* sent us to lodgings at an old church that had been turned into a dorm for volunteers after the 1966 flood. We paid a little more than $3 a night for one layer each in a 3-person bunk bed. We heard there are beautiful frescoes in some of the dorm rooms." ... "Today we honored Michelangelo and went to the Academy Gallery, the Buonarotti house, and Santa Croce. The *David* is so alive and beautiful that I waited for him to move and almost thought I could smell his body. I looked at the bust of Michelangelo trying to see the genius in his face. No luck." ... "Saw Donatello's *David*s, but I knew that no matter how long I waited, they would never breathe like Buonarotti's beautiful boy does." ... "In a coffee shop this morning, a man saw my peace button and spoke with Carolyn while I was in the john. '*Pacifista?*' he asked her. She said 'yes,' and he pointed at himself and said '*communista.*' He told us he had fought the fascists and showed us a certificate he'd been given by the Allied Forces for service." ... "We heard an oncoming roar, and suddenly the street in front of our dormitory was filled with students demonstrating in support of students rioting now in Mexico."

Train to Toulouse: "We were living on raspberry hard candies because we didn't want to convert any more currency to *lira*. A cute Frenchman in our compartment jokingly proposed marriage, but all I was thinking of was Roquefort cheese and French bread." ... "By 7 a.m. we were waiting for the ticket office to open at the Toulouse rail station so we could buy tickets and get to Auch in time for the work camp. Our Eurail passes will expire at midnight."

Auch: "We made it! But since we don't have to be at the work camp until Friday, and since everything seems better after a rest, we stayed in Auch in a shabby little hotel for under $2 each." ... "The French love when I use even my poor French to speak with them. Today, over my protests of not speaking well, an elderly shopkeeper said, '*Mais, vous comprenez bien. Vous comprenez tres bien!*' " ... "Everywhere we go, people ask if we're English. When we tell them we're American and are here to '*faire le vendange*,' they tell us we're '*courageuses*' and '*bien loin de la maison.*' " … "On a walk outside town, we ran into a young man we'd met at a café our first night here. He was adamant that we'd not seen enough of Toulouse and asked us to go there for dinner that night. He and a friend, both soldiers, arrived all dressed up and off we went to a seafood restaurant in Toulouse. Our three-hour meal included oysters, prawns, clams, mussels, little snails, big snails, bean and sausage casserole, white and red wine, and ice cream. One of my snails was red, and Claude asked, 'What did you say to him to make him blush like that?' The road back to Auch ran through dark, empty countryside that stretched for miles with only the light of the moon. I was nervous, but the young men were good people. We even stopped at a little club out in the middle of the fields to have a drink and dance for a while."

Eauze: "We took a bus to Eauze in the morning but once there found out that the bus to Castelnau leaves from a different town. It was time to regroup over a cup of coffee. Not many Americans come through Eauze, and the tavern proprietor was chatty and friendly. When he understood our situation, he insisted on calling the farm where we will work, and M. Dumon, the agricultural engineer who owns the farm, came and picked us up."

Castelnau-d'Auzan 10/11-10/25: "There is no work camp, and they have already hired some Romani to pick the grapes. Our fate and that of the other 16 young people sent by Concordia will be decided tomorrow, when we'll be timed against the pros. Two young French guys who are sons of Dumon friends will pick, too." … "We've been kept, but the Romani left after a battle royal about how much food Mme. Dumon was giving them. Our foreman, Andre, carried his hunting rifle all day in the vineyard." … "There are 12 Czechs, two

Germans, an Englishman, and a young French woman here in addition to me and Carolyn. Except for the French guys, who sleep in the farmhouse with the family, we're all sleeping in an outbuilding on frames covered with bags of straw. Two rooms for the girls, one room for the guys. No toilets. Surprising how well we can pee off a step or out a window!"
... "Our communal meals are in the 300-year-old farmhouse under open beams hung with curing hams. The Dumons are wealthy and have a new home in Agen and a small house in Biarritz, but they run the *vendange* with great practicality. Mme. said they have not earned one franc from the farm in 10 years but keep it because they love the property.

La Petite Maison—Our Quarters

Photo by Carolyn S. Carr

She said DeGaulle favors industry over agriculture. Mme. wears a silk blouse and beautifully tailored slacks when she cooks our meals in the kitchen with Sylvette, the farm foreman's wife. Mme. always looks jaunty because she has a long cigarette holder with a Gauloise sticking out of her mouth at a 45-degree angle all day. The kitchen is in action the whole time we are picking grapes. Their workday runs from

Andre, Our Foreman, with Breakfast Bread

Photo by Carolyn S. Carr

7am to 10pm preparing meals for the 18 of us and cleaning up after. Mme. works all day." ... "We eat our whole meal, soup to dessert, from one dish each. Bits of my fish remained in my chocolate pudding tonight. Bottles of white wine are on the table at every meal, even breakfast, but the wine is raw stuff and is supposed to be cut with water. At breakfast we also have bowls of coffee and hot milk, with slices from huge loaves of bread that we spread with butter and honey. At every meal, the table is a Babel of English, Czech, French, Spanish, and German, with conversations and cross-translations going on in all five languages."

... "Our schedule on six days of the week (Sundays off) is: 7am get up; 8am breakfast; work from 9am to 1pm, when M. Jean, our elderly *chef de travail*, yells '*a la soupe*'; lunch with wine then a lie down until 2:30; back to work until 6 then supper. Not a grueling schedule, but the grapes are heavy, and after my first day picking them, I fell asleep halfway through writing a sentence in my journal. Andre said they will send me home '*tres forte*.' " ... "Opened my eyes at 7am, and already the Czechs were talking politics, also in the vineyards and at lunch and at supper and during the evening." ... "In the afternoon, I was sitting on a stool washing underpants at an outdoor tap when one of the Czechs, Lubosch, requested a performance of 'We Shall Overcome.' I obliged as I scrubbed. Later, Lubosch asked us to teach all the Czechs. Now we sing

Monsieur Jean, Our Chef de Travail

Photo by Carolyn S. Carr

Lubosch: "mo-MENT!"
Photo by Carolyn S. Carr

it as we pick grapes and at supper." … "Today I've had to answer questions from the Czechs about both the Court of Appeals and our drug problem in the States; they say they have neither. When Lubosch, who's becoming our best friend here, doesn't understand an explanation, he pushes his glasses back up his nose and loudly demands a pause, '*mo*-MENT, Leen, *mo*-MENT, Caroleen.' " … "Carolyn got so sick she was moved to the big house, and I stayed with her there. I worked in the kitchen for three days so I could bring meals to her and not disturb Marie, the elderly maid." … "Peder explained *The Dharma Bums* as 'people with dangerous anti-group tendencies' " … "Each country sang its national anthem at dinner, and the Czechs wept as they sang. Lubosch told us how he saw his best friend and a 5-year-old kid shot dead when the Czechs threw stones at Russian soldiers entering his town near the border. Although he knows the word 'shot' (his English is good), he just said, 'POM POM POM.' When he wanted to say someone was sent to forced labor, he crossed his hands over his face like bars and said nothing." … "Bowls of chicken blood in the kitchen—later, fried and sliced, it resembled liver, but I couldn't manage to eat any at supper." … "Norbert, one of the Germans, gathered chestnuts in the farmyard and roasted them for all of us in the fireplace coals at our little house." … "Lubosch translated the title of the Salinger book he's read, *Catcher in the Rye*, as *Who Is Catching in the Cereals*. I laughed so hard I fell off my cot." … "The cop I was dating sent me the PBA report on the Newark riots. I tried not to read it in front of the Czechs because they're so curious about the States. I could never explain the riots to them in French or German." … "The farm has 17 acres of vineyards. We've now reached about 25 barrels a day picking. The barrels are huge and hold about 500 or 600 kilos of grapes each, which will make about 400 liters of wine. The wine is usually about 18 proof but this year's wine won't be, M. Jean said, because the grapes are not great and the wine will be too sweet. The wine is for local consumption. What the village co-op distills and sells is Armagnac brandy. They find it odd that they sell so little in the States, but their representative is in Dayton, Ohio!" ... "Jean Louis, one of the French guys, predicted a race problem in France with Arabs in the distant future. He also said Gaullist candidates won the French elections on a reactionary tide after the May Disorders. Mme. said France would be better if DeGaulle were dead. She said great upheavals would follow, but when they were over, progress could go on." ... "Carolyn and I pelted Lubosch with grapes—'You dirty communist,' we yelled--as we rode back to the farmhouse on the flatbed. Andre drove the tractor that pulled us, and Philippe and Jean Louis rode the tractor like a horse. We bombed them with grapes, too. We were happy because we'd finished a day of hard work. The locals work hard all their lives. Arthritis and rheumatism seem common. And M. Jean coughs a lot. He said it's from *le gaz* in the First World War, but the damp roll-your-own cigarettes

Madame Herbay, Giselle's Mother

Photo by Carolyn S. Carr

always hanging from his lips must help it along." ... "I was looking at Jean Louis's long, tan body and his big handsome Gallic features, and my mind strayed. In the dirt and fatigue, I've forgotten I'm a woman, forgotten all the lovely touches, smells, and sounds of love. My hands are cut up and filthy with ground-in dirt. I'm a grape-picking machine, and even sleep is such a necessity that its beauty is lost." … "Lubosch held up his passport. 'Leetle man, leetle passport, leetle country,' he said then pointed at me and Carolyn. 'Beeg girl. Beeg passport. Beeg country.' Then he taught us the Czech words for 'little man': *maly muz*." … "Giselle has offered us a ride to her home in Nemours, which will save us 2/3 of our trip back to Luxembourg. We can auto-stop from Nemours." … "*Hloopy* means 'silly' in Czech, and we are hloopier and hloopier as the end of our *vendange* nears. We all *chatouillions* [tickle] each other and launch ambushes with glasses of water." … "The *vendange* ends tomorrow, but some of the Czechs have already left. Lubosch has to get to Dijon for a cousin's wedding, so he woke us at 5am to say goodbye and make us promise to visit Czechoslovakia next year. His toast at dinner last night was 'to capitalist girls!' Supper started with six bottles of wine on the table and accelerated." …"Carolyn and I picked our last row of grapevines. After lunch, we went into the dining room for our wages from Mme. The three of us agreed that we weren't the fastest pickers here and settled on 15 francs a day (about $3) with 9 francs subtracted for our meals on Sundays off. Everyone else was either in town or picking corn for some extra money, so Carolyn and I took over the tank in the barn for a hot bath. We could smell the cows, and there were chicken feathers floating in the water, but the pleasure of that bath is beyond my power to describe." … "A letter to Carolyn from the States upset me. Her friend said we should stay here, that the left and right are diverging further and becoming dogmatic and dictatorial as their ranks galvanize. The friend has joined the [Eugene] McCarthy movement to reform from within." … "As Giselle drove us toward Nemours, the sky darkened and it got cold. She announced that we would not auto-stop tonight but would sleep at her house and leave tomorrow. I welcomed this especially because along the way I vomited up last night's goose dinner and didn't feel tiptop." … "The Herbays warmly made room for two American strays. Giselle's pet fox, Gaspard, lives in the barn and growled when we vis-

The Whole Vendange Crew by Carolyn

ited him. 'He's forgotten me,' she said. Over supper, the family asked about Jaqueline Kennedy's marriage to Aristotle Onassis. They're puzzled by it as were many of the French we've met. Giselle's mother also told us that Lyndon Johnson has scheduled a special press conference where people expect him to announce the cessation of the bombing of North Vietnam. At bedtime, we grabbed our sleeping bags, but Mme. Herbay insisted on a freshly made bed with clean linen sheets. Giselle left us a bucket for a toilet. In the morning, we lay in bed smoking and talking about home. It's time to return. After breakfast, Giselle drove us to an approach road for the A6. We put out our thumbs, and a truck stopped. The driver tossed our backpacks into the rear, and off we went, back to Paris. At Gare de l'Est, we got second-class tickets for the slow train to Luxembourg."

On the train: " 'What do you think Lubosch is doing now?' I asked Carolyn. 'He's at his cousin's wedding, probably drunk, and singing "We Shall Overcome." After which he will say, "THAT is a good protest song!' "

Luxembourg: "We got in after midnight, rented a hotel room near the station for a little over $5 for the two of us, went to a nearby bar for a snack, and did a bit of laundry in the sink. Plans for tomorrow are sleep, sleep, sleep." ... "After supper, the Loftleidir office was still open, and with great jollification we reserved two seats on Flight 401-403 to New York. We have enough money to buy the airline's 2-day package in Iceland—all-inclusive for $34! We'll get to New York November 1 at 7am, and we wired our parents the information."

Iceland: "We have visibility of 90 miles from our Reykyavik hotel because there is so little air pollution. The city is heated by its hot springs and there is a 200 per cent import duty on cars. I sampled creamy *skyr* at breakfast and fishy whale meat at lunch. Our guide pointed out a 60-year-old stand of trees that are about three feet high—such a spare land. We saw lava fields, spouting geysers, and hot mud pools." ... "Carolyn bought me an ashtray made of lava. It has the Helmet of Terror rune on it and comes with the following instructions from Viking times: 'This symbol you shall place between your eyebrows with your right ring finger, using blood drawn from your own body; thereafter will you go fearless against your enemies.' But what if you are, like me, your own worst enemy?"

Flying Home: "We channeled Flip Wilson. 'Gonna go to America! Gonna find Ray Charles!' " ... "And on the plane, nerves, nerves, nerves that have gone so far now that even we have both lost our appetites."

Home: "After we'd been home a few days, Carolyn called. 'When are you coming to Connecticut to see me?' 'How about yesterday?' I answered." ... "People ask why I went. People ask why I came back. I have no explanation. I went to see the world. And Dad says you always come back."

So I came back to my parents' house and Edgewater, and when the *Dispatch* learned that I was home and asked me to come back to work there, I said yes. But this time I was honest and told them I'd be applying to other newspapers while I worked for them.

An Alphabet of Guys

E is for Engaged

(Soundtrack: *Rock the Boat* by The Hues Corporation)

So, the two guys I was dating show up—separately—to welcome me back from Europe. One's a chaotic charmer, the returned high school boyfriend I'd been thinking about maybe marrying when I got back. He greets me by dragging in the door and saying he's tired. The other is the policeman, E, the one I played Catch the Marijuana with many miles and months before. "How was Europe?" he asks and gives me a big grin. I choose the policeman.

He has red hair and blue eyes like my father. He was born, raised, and still lives in my dad's hometown. Eventually we'll plan to marry in my dad's old parish. At the time, I see all this as coincidence. E is older than me, but it's only by six years, hardly a father figure, right?

My mother really likes this new relationship. E's job requires that he always carry his gun. So the daughter that she has worried over since birth now travels with her own armed guard.

E appreciates that I'm not like the other cops' girlfriends and wives. He tends to go his own way, too. He's not tough or cynical, and he views with kindness most of what he sees on the job. I'm also not like his family; his and his brothers' lives are more like my dad's generation. And while I *am* a redhead like *his* mom, she's tiny and quiet and capable, and I'm, well, bigger, melodramatic, and still kind of unstable. E is the kind of cop who has a heart full of help for people. He thinks he can file down my sharp edges just a bit. Then I will be both the woman he finds interesting and the woman he wants to settle down with; we'll share a happy life. Although he likes some edge, he hasn't really taken the full measure of mine. He's not stupid, but he is a kind and optimistic man.

We both still live with our parents; this makes sex problematic. And there's another problem. He seems willing to wait for sex, and I find that odd. Our make-out sessions are hot, which is promising, but I'd like to know how we go the distance before I do anything official. So I push for that, and it turns out that night clerks at motels are very accommodating to cops. We try that once. It's OK. Then I borrow a friend's empty apartment in New York. It's OK again. So we get engaged, announce it in the newspaper, and receive a set of stainless steel bowls from my grandmother. My mom and I even buy a hope chest. This is going to be very traditional. I hardly know myself …

… until I do again. On one night that we have a date, a favorite dress doesn't fit when I try it on. I hate myself when I feel fat, and when I hate myself, I destroy things. So, I grab each side of the neckline and yank the dress in two. Downstairs, E and my mother are in the living room talking. Their conversation halts when they hear my howls of outrage and the noise of ripping seams and fabric from my room. There may also be some stomping on the floor. The crazy noises are hard enough to ignore, but then stuff starts flying down the stairs into the living room. I hurl pieces of the dress, the shoes I'd planned to wear, and a necklace. Conversation is no longer possible.

E doesn't back out of our engagement that night. I finally find something to wear, and we go out. But he has begun to see that I'm too much crazy for him, and he makes his case. "… real differences in our personalities … I won't be able to make you happy … not sure we want the same things …" We part ways. I'm not particularly unhappy, but my mother is disappointed: he would have been such a safe place to store me. But my lack of heartache says something undeniable, and years later, after I finally meet the man I need, she will say, "It's good that it ended with E. You would have gotten bored and you would have hurt the both of you."

F Is for Furious
(Soundtrack: *Whole Lotta Love* by Led Zeppelin)

I always knew as soon as I saw them. Most were tall, long-haired, and usually wearing old Levis. They had slow, knowing walks, and I knew at first glance that I wanted them. I don't grow into these things.

So, I'm at a party in the Flats one cold Edgewater evening and F walks in. The host is a friend of my friend and F is a friend of the host. A few apartments in the Flats have passed from working-class families to young people from outside town who want a cheap place to live near Manhattan. I am in the hallway of the railroad flat when F comes through the door. He says hi to a guy I don't know, and the guy puts a pill in his hand. F pops it in his mouth without a glance and washes it down with some of the guy's beer. I'm astounded that he doesn't care what the pill is. I have only recently been engaged to a cop, and from F I catch a whiff of risk that interests me more now than law and order.

I keep my eye on him. He's tall and big boned, not from the Irish side of his family, I will learn. His size is from the Hungarian side. His fingers are long and graceful as he repeatedly twines a lock of brown hair back behind his ear. I smile. He smiles. We wander separately around the flat, but we are careful to end up in the same rooms. Eventually we talk. I like his voice; it's deep and smooth. We drink cheap wine. We join conversations and drift away again. After a while we hold hands. And when it's very late and we are tired, he says, "Don't leave." We get a blanket and roll up in it on the kitchen floor somewhere out of the way. As the tempo of the party winds down around us, we fall asleep.

***

We stay together for two years in spite of our limitations. He introduces me to some new music—Fred Neil, Led Zeppelin, the Allman Brothers, and the Grateful Dead. We go to see the Dead at midnight at the Fillmore East and leave the theater at dawn, dancing in East Village streets that are still empty. He likes modernist architecture, so we prowl the Seagram Building and steal from a lobby table a big designer ashtray of chrome and black enamel. I still have it, though no one I know smokes anymore. Back then, everyone did.

We don't have much spare cash, so we spend time just roaming Manhattan or the banks of the Hudson. "Le Corbusier loved the George Washington Bridge," F tells me. "He used to sit on the New York side and look at it for hours." I can appreciate that. After growing up at the bridge's feet, I was disappointed when I finally saw the Golden Gate. Painted in what looked to me like primer coat, it didn't have the gravitas of the Great Gray Bridge. F also starts me reading Thomas Pynchon. His deeply laid conspiracies appeal to F's sense of the times. "They're building secret camps out west to put us in when they round us up," he tells me. Although I doubt that, it's second nature to feel targeted. We're drinking in a Teaneck bar when we watch the draft lottery on TV. Voices in the bar are stilled; the only noise comes from the blue lottery capsules clicking against each other and a man's voice calling out the birth date contained in each capsule drawn. F's number is high; he's safe, but we have friends who drug themselves before draft physicals or find anti-war shrinks to certify them unfit.

As for our individual limitations, mine is what it has always been, the deep conviction that I'm not lovable, a conviction that makes me doubt almost anything positive that happens between us. Sometimes I'm mute with anxiety or anger, neither of which I understand. "What are you thinking?" he asks when I'm silent. I feel like I don't know, but, in fact, I refuse to know, and eventually this resistance angers him. F says to give in to the unexplored parts of my mind. "You know them already if they're part of you. Just go into them." But this comes from a man who can swallow any pill handed to him and keep on rolling. I still need to avoid my deepest unexplored places.

Because what we are together is risky and undefined for me, I can't, don't, won't initiate sex, even though I'm always happy when he does. I love the sound of his voice when it's pitched low and the sight of his tall, naked body. "Why don't you ever seduce me?" he asks. If I'd answer, and of course I don't, I'd say, "Because you don't love me, and I don't want to act the fool." One day, exasperated, he says, "Do you want me to say 'I love you'? OK, then, I love you." Not a ringing endorsement, but even if it had been, I would have remained unconvinced. Not all my reasons for feeling that way are subjective. His old girlfriends sometimes turn up at his apartment or call him. But I don't ask questions.

He knows that he's troubled, too. He lost direction, he tells me, when he was 14, and his mother sickened from cancer. He swears she passed over him in bed at home at the moment she died in the hospital. He's been in freefall ever since. His father remarried, but F didn't like the woman and often stayed at friends' houses. He finished high school but he keeps quitting college. He doesn't really live anywhere but stays sometimes at his father's house, sometimes in friends' apartments or dorm rooms. Eventually he and a friend get a 3-room apartment in Fort Lee. F's room is the living room and he puts a mattress on the floor. He takes low-skill jobs, like moving boxes in an archive or manning a high-rise reception desk at night. At jobs like those, he can read a lot and wear his basic wardrobe of blue jeans, a work shirt, and a pea jacket. He quits the jobs once he qualifies for unemployment.

Although I feel unlovable and F is headed nowhere, together we manage to do me one huge favor. We decide to move in together. Or, more accurately, I push to move in together and he agrees. I'm back to seeing the shrink, and he's encouraging me to stand on my own more. By now, I'm working at the *Bergen Record* so I have a salary. At 24, he says, I should not still be living with my parents. I doubt that he thinks F is a good alternative, but he is the alternative I have and he's a step in the right direction, away from being a child in my parents' home.

We find a cheap apartment in Ridgefield Park, and I make all my preparations without mentioning to my parents that I'll be living there with F. At every session, my shrink asks if I've told them yet. My "no" lands like a lead sinker each time. He only asks and says nothing further, but I know he won't let me slip-slide around the issue. His question is back again at the next session. When I finally decide to force-march myself through an announcement, I also decide to go for broke and approach my father alone, before I tell my mother.

It's past time for me to complete a confrontation with my father uninterrupted. My mother has always stepped in to defuse them. After her mother's death, my mother fitted herself into other people's households. Whether she was a boarder or living with a stepmother or taken in by a sister's family, those places were not hers in the way most mothers make a home for their own children. She fit into them by avoiding conflict. So, in our family, when my father and I start to fight, she draws the issue to herself. "The two of you will drive me to Greystone," she announces tearfully. So he and I are partnered then, not at odds. We retreat to our separate corners, and quiet—if not calm—prevails.

This time I'm determined to see a conflict through with my father. When he goes down into the cellar, I follow him and close the door after me. I'm too nervous for a preamble.

"I'm moving into the apartment with F," I say to his back.

He stops walking. Silence. He turns slowly toward me and stares. A long stare. Then he heads past me back upstairs, his chore abandoned.

"You'll never convince *me*," he says over his shoulder.

"I don't want to convince you," I say to his back. "I just want you to know who I am."

He leaves the house quietly. Then I tell my mother.

"I'm moving into that apartment with F. I just told Daddy."

"Oh, no" she moans and runs after him. They return in a half hour, and nothing more is said about it by any of us.

I have been brave enough to march myself through the announcement, but that night, I get scared. I go to a friend's house and stay over. I'm back home the next night but sleep with my bureau in front of my bedroom door. I have announced my independence and my sexuality and I think my dad might kill me.

Days pass and nothing happens. Eventually I leave the bureau in its regular place at night. We three say nothing about my plans. "I'm sad that you and Daddy aren't speaking to each other," my mother tells me one day. "We're not?" I say. My surprise is genuine. Our conversation seems to me as frequent as it's always been.

I move into the new, shared apartment, and the arrangement lasts about six months. One day I answer the phone and it is yet again the girlfriend from just before me calling. She's fine telling me who it is. "Have you been seeing her?" I ask when he hangs up. "Yeah."

Something flashes through me and I grab drinking glasses and start throwing them at the kitchen wall. Some are heavy beer mugs, and if I throw one and it doesn't break, I pick it up and throw it over and over until it does. I hear my outraged howls as if they come from someone else. Finally I up and wallop him on the shoulder once.

"I've been fucked up since my mother died," he says.

Somehow that steadies me.

"Stop blaming her," I say. "And get the fuck out."

He does get out. Later that day, I stack all his stuff in the yard.

Yet again I'm tumbling through space. I feel like I don't exist. I'm alone and unloved. The grief and humiliation are overwhelming, and I can't get myself out the door. So I miss days of work before my friend Nora comes over. "You're going to be docked pay," she says, "and, if you don't get your shit together soon, you'll be fired." So I drag myself to the newspaper office and force myself to interview people and write stories.

***

"I threw glasses and punched him. I acted crazy," I tell my shrink at our next meeting.

"Sounds to me like you finally acted sane," he says.

It's the last time I lose my self in a breakup.

***

Maybe eight months later, I go to an open house party in Edgewater in the big old apartment building on the corner of Dempsey Avenue and River Road. It turns out to be an apartment F shares with some other guys. We talk like old friends, and he says he's missed me. When the apartment empties out in the very early morning hours, he says once again, "Don't leave." It doesn't have the sexy edge of the first time he said it. Maybe he just doesn't want to be alone. And I stay because I wonder what I will feel about all this. By dawn, his breathing is deep and regular, and I slip out of his bed. We're over. I know I want to leave. Outside the dawn light is delicate. River Road is still empty, and the Hudson has the soft glow of silver. A breeze blows off the river, and life seems full of possibility.

G Is for Golden

(Soundtrack: *Catch the Wind* by The Blues Project)

G travels in some of the same circles as F does, but I don't meet him until after F and I split up. G has a wife somewhere, or maybe she's an ex-wife, or maybe they aren't actually married. She has kids, and some of them are G's, or maybe just one of them, or maybe none of them. G is a mystery and a wanderer. He is also a drinker and a doper. By the time I meet him, he seems to have done more dope than anyone else I know. He's intelligent and a reader who's fun to talk with until his train of thought hits a short-circuited synapse. Then silence descends for minutes or hours until he is, once again, back in the world.

He's medium height and medium build, closer to my size than my usual choice in guys. What attracts me is the warm light of him. Gold glints in his light brown hair. The pupils of his eyes have the same tiny bits of gold. He looks like a small, sturdy lion in afternoon sunlight. He even smells warm, like beach sand in August. And I buy into his beauty and his chaos as I did with other men. But something has changed in me.

Skin Deep

> I will let myself feel you
> On my first layer of skin.
> I have only seven
> And won't be flayed again.
> I'm done tending
> Muscles, lacy nerves, blood vessels, and organs,
> Deep and glistening parts of me
> Left exposed
> To the dry air,
> To the drying light
> By a careless man.
> This much I will give us,

One layer,
For your lion's eyes,
Just one.

Magician

Wrapped in nomads' desert tents,
The bright stripes billowing in the wind,
You perform The Great Disappearing Act.
The moon, the sun, and the stars
Will come out
When the magician reappears.
But since you left,
I ate oranges
And drank coffee.
I used soap scented with apricots
Then ran my nose across my skin
To smell them.
I stayed in a cabin in the woods
And opened Christmas presents by the ocean.
I owned a dog and
She was wolf-like and beautiful.
I read books
And painted the bathroom bright blue.
Day after day
The plants in my windows slowly grew.
When you reappeared, hey presto!
You knew nothing about the oranges, the cabin, or the wolf-dog.

***

My friend Nora and I are standing in the brightly lit city room when she asks, "Have you heard from G?"

"No, he's still in Israel," I say.

"He's not. He came back two weeks ago."

I wait for the familiar sensation of falling and the fear that it unleashes. And I do fall a bit, a small jolt like when an elevator re-adjusts at a new floor. But something comes up under me, some sense of solid ground. I feel that lovely, chaotic G, the wanderer and doper, is about himself, not about me. His affection has been real and his chaos has been real, and I know little to nothing about either of those things in him. I will miss him, but I do not feel shamed or unmoored or invisible.

***

"At last we have an ego," my shrink says when I tell him what has happened and how I felt. He usually says very little during a session and what he does say is generally a question. "How did you feel about that?" "What were you just thinking?" "Why do you think you did that?" And he has never slipped into Freudian speak before. It's a strong and unusual pronouncement from him.

H Is for Hiker

(Soundtrack: *Keep a Knockin'* by Little Richard)

H is a reporter at the *Bergen Record* where I work. By the time I start seeing him, I'm enjoying my life with good friends and a job that I love. The paper has made a transition to a Lifestyle section. Our managing editor says, "I hear the way you girls [sic] talk at lunch. I want you to write that way now." So, led by the models of New Journalism and the *Washington Post* Style section, we add a world of description to our articles. Adjectives, adverbs, and some *mise en scene* enter. We are staff *writers*. We get to cover issues in the news like abortion and the Equal Rights Amendment. New York City is nearby, and there we interview writers, musicians, and actors. We gin up features on places in the city we're curious about. We are having *fun*, and my bosses think I'm good at this.

By now, I feel deeply planted. Therapy, journalism, and Europe have formed ground I can stand on, "an ego" in my shrink's words. From now on, sex will be for fun. No more years spent with men I should only have slept with a few times. If something deeper—whatever that means—comes along, well, who knows what happens? In the meantime, my life is full.

For a while, H feels like someone who might go deep. We share teasing, affectionate conversations. He *does* things, and we have fun doing them together. He knows the hiking trails in Rockland and Orange Counties, and we go hiking often enough that I buy sturdy leather boots. We cook together, too. We start at the good Italian grocery store in Hackensack and make our plan as we walk the aisles. Broiled steaks and steamed artichokes. Or ingredients for spaghetti sauce. Or maybe for a ricotta cheesecake. We cook at my apartment, and, after we eat, we walk the train tracks in the Meadowlands behind where I live. Lights twinkle all over a huge Public Service generating plant in the distance. It reminds me of the castle of Ming the Merciless from *Flash Gordon*. The shopping then cooking then eating then making love then sleeping fill a Sunday. He stays overnight, and we have to rush to work the next morning.

H is a gift giver, too, surprise gifts for no occasion. That's new for me: pastel argyle socks shot through with sparkly Lurex threads, a thrift shop handbag covered in cloth flowers, a Lucite trivet with real tea cookies and wildflowers trapped inside. I like his gifts and I feel understood by him because his choices please me.

But the relationship has an expiry date.

My friend Nora is, as usual, clear-eyed and frank.

"Life hangs on him like that tweed jacket he wears."

He's prone to discouragement and pessimism like I am. Nora doubts that we will bring out the best in each other.

* * *

"We're better friends now and worse lovers," I say to him one night in bed.

"It's always like that eventually, isn't it?" H answers.

And I think, *No, I won't accept that.*

For H—4/73

I stand on the bank
And I watch what is you flow past.
But let me step off
And into the current
To ask,
"What is this
You are?"
And a ripple breaks around my ankles
With a murmur of protest.
You flow on
And leave me
On dry land wondering.

Newspapers Deliver

Journalism let me earn a living reading and writing, the things I most enjoy doing in this world. It plunked me down into newsrooms that were full of playful, smart, eccentric people. It made me learn how to engage with strangers, so my interviews could produce compelling stories. It let me cherry-pick opportunities to interview interesting people (Bette Davis! Allen Ginsberg! Estelle Parsons!) and to write about topics that were important to me (second-wave feminism! Zero Population Growth! the spring shad run in Edgewater!). Then, one busy morning in the city room, journalism brought me another gift.

All the Rest Is with Marc

(Soundtrack: *Here Comes the Sun* by The Beatles)

My dad, the adventurer, had trouble with intimacy. My mom, the nurturer, needed me to stay safe. But I wanted adventure and intimacy, excitement and a nurturing love. For years, I slept with men like my father and felt I wanted them to change. In fact, I was caught in a loop. They attracted me because they were leery of intimacy like my dad was. You can call this repetition compulsion; Freud did.

> *Repetition compulsion is a psychological phenomenon in which a person repeats an event or its circumstances over and over again. This includes re-enacting the event or putting oneself in situations where the event is likely to happen again. ... Traumatic repetitions could be seen as the result of an attempt to retrospectively "master" the original*

> *trauma, a child's play as an attempt to turn passivity into activity ...*
>
> Wikipedia

The behavior puzzled Freud because it contradicts the pleasure principle: 'If it feels good, I want to do it. If it feels bad, I don't want to," my words, not Freud's. But compulsion has its own principles: Even if it feels bad, it feels normal. And, even if it feels bad, maybe this time the same behavior will result in a different outcome. The men I chose and the way I behaved with them fit my deepest sense of what I was, unlovable, and what would happen to me, abandonment ... but maybe next time, I'd power through to happiness and solve the puzzle life had handed me.

Uh, no.

While I was stuck in that behavior, adventure and commitment would remain mutually exclusive. But after six years of therapy and in that small, new space that opened between me and G, I finally separated from the compulsion and could make different choices. Then I was ready to meet Marc and to make something of the opportunity.

* * *

My usually clear-eyed friend Nora was initially fooled by Marc's personality. His cheery energy looked to her like innocence. She warned me that Marc, though only three years younger, was too young for me. She'd seen me through some funky, low moments and did not think that cheery energy was the sea I could swim in. For once, she was wrong. I had changed and I was ready. And although he was cheery, he was not uncomplicated. Over the years together that followed, like all couples, we had to deal with whatever hungry ghosts still haunted each of us. Fights got loud. I broke stuff. Worse yet, sometimes I withdrew.   On one vacation, I ran away for a day. He sulked when we fought. We both indulged in long, sullen silences. The ghosts were challenging, but we like to talk, which helped because exorcising ghosts takes years of talking, with a shrink or with a partner.

We began a conversation on the chilly March night we first spoke in 1974. A friend at the paper where we worked threw a dinner party just to get us to the same table. I'd been watching this bushy-haired, bearded cutie in the city room, and Carol had run out of patience listening to me talk about him. I made the most of the opportunity she gave me and grabbed the seat next to him at dinner. We talked through the evening, and after we left the party, we went for a walk along the Hudson from the Edgewater Colony, just south of the bridge, to the Englewood Boat Basin. The air was clear and the lights on both shores and the bridge were bright. It was a beautiful night. As we walked north, we talked, and after an hour, when we turned back, we were still talking. We ate breakfast at the Fort Lee Diner and kissed good night in the parking lot there. The conversation continued by phone from home and then back at work, and it continues now, more than four decades later. "I fell in love with you," he told me, "that night we walked along the river."

The Weaver

> The craving to connect
> Jams
> In my throat.
> I refuse
> To risk
> Making a claim for
> Your attention.
> My face fails me.
> The yielding look
> I give you

When you've gone
Is tight as sunburn
When we are
Face to face.

But I have moments.
Some threads I lightly throw
Are caught—what? —
I find myself
Tied in odd places.
My words, heard,
Fit here and now—laughter.
Some needs known. How?
You hear years, catch
The threads I toss,
Weave them
Into patterns of
A syntax tying me to you.

Comforting the Creature

Marc wasn't shaken when I sobbed after the first time we made love. He accepted the tears and just held me. The discouraged creature within me no longer felt alone, and relief overwhelmed me. I began to let go of an exorbitant loneliness.

"I Love You"

You can long for deep love and commitment for years while remaining threatened by them. You can solve that paradox by believing that you are simply not lovable. And you can do all that blind to the choices you make that guarantee failure.

"I think I'm going to throw up," I answered the first time Marc said he loved me. He laughed. Then I laughed. He was only 25, but he was there. If I stretched out a hand or tossed a thought to him, he was *there*. My hand or my thought encountered something willing and complex that responded honestly. And because he was there, I was there in new ways. The change was dizzying. Whatever happened between us would be intimate and real. No hiding. And that was what made my stomach lurch.

For Marc

>Windows fly open.
>Curtains belly out
>In the morning air.
>Pale light
>Outlines with precision
>The objects in the bedroom.
>Windows fly open.
>Things fall
>Into gentle disorder.
>Knots fly apart
>And windows fly open.

How Enough Feels

Something odd happened then. I stopped fantasizing about the relationship I was in. I no longer dreamt about possible futures together. Each day with Marc was full. Each moment in itself was enough.

What a Woman Wants

First I had to believe I deserved it. Next I had to believe it existed. Then I could find it:

> *A man who takes care of himself and others with grace*
> *A man who is not afraid of women*
> *A man who is not looking for a mother*
> *A man who makes interesting plans and follows through on them*
> *A man with laugh wrinkles at the corners of his eyes*
> *A man who doesn't need alcohol*
> *A man who protects the people he loves but even more often challenges them*
> *A man who enjoys his work*
> *A man who says "I'm sorry" and means it*
> *A man who hears "I'm sorry" and believes it*
> *A man who knows that being alive is worth all the work it takes to do it well*

That does it nicely for me. And what did Marc want? That's his story to tell.

Marc and I on Our Wedding Day

Photo by Irving Kaufman

The Recipe

This is how I saved my life. First, I embraced therapy. I embraced it out of desperation, but I embraced it. Second, newspapers found me. I had no agency in that beyond knowing I loved them once they *had* found me. Third, I got on that plane with Carolyn. Each step took me back into the world.

My River Town Changed, Too

Edgewater was a town of two-family houses, a few apartment buildings, and some small stores when I was a kid. Its size was well scaled to people. I knew who lived in almost every building I walked past and who owned all the stores. There were 4,000 or so residents then.

Every Friday, my mom bought meat at the shop on Hilliard Avenue owned by Tom Zaia, a butcher with justifiable confidence in his product. Even a kid like me could see the conviction with which he slapped cuts down on the worn butcher's block. They would be tender (the only kind my dad would eat), or you could return them. Mr. Zaia knew *that* was not going to happen. Next, Mom got our produce just up the block at Chick Criscuolo's store. Later his brother, Joe, took over the small market. For a short season every year, kids bypassed the candy store and instead bought pomegranates at Criscuolo's with our after-school snack money. Mr. Bernath was a tailor on that same street. His daughter Gloria was in my class. I wasn't in his shop much because my mother did our sewing.

Also on Hilliard Avenue was a cobbler whose name I can't remember, but I can picture sitting with my mother in one of the waist-high booths in his shop. Each wooden booth had a swinging door to it and a bench inside upholstered in red leather. What strange modesty required a private place for our stockinged feet? I didn't ask. I just waited on the bench with my mother as the cobbler re-heeled her shoes or put metal taps on mine.

The town had one chain store then, a small A&P with slow ceiling fans and wood floors worn into shallow dips at the heavily trafficked places. But Mom liked Packard Bamberger's in Hackensack better than A&P, so my dad drove us there every Friday night for the cleaning supplies, cooking ingredients, and candy on her list. Our Friday night expedition got shorter when Food Fair opened in Fort Lee.

Now there are big chain stores in Edgewater. Whole Foods and Trader Joe's have built along the river. I try to imagine what Edgewater's children will remember of those places 60 years from now. Will they buy after-school pomegranates at Whole Foods? Will they know the produce man's name? Will they go to school with his kids? And where has the cobbler gone? Are the children's worn shoes just thrown into the garbage? Of course they are. What would a cobbler do with the worn rubber sole of a Nike? In the 1950s, with just 4,000-plus residents, the streets crawled with kids. Are many kids out on those streets now that the town has 12,000 residents?

An article in the *New York Times* real estate section on June 7, 2017, cites the housing Web site Neighborhood Scout, which reports that 78 percent of housing in Edgewater was built after 1969. Maybe that explains the *Times*'s characterization of my hometown as a "conventional suburb." It certainly wasn't conventional or a suburb when I lived there.

Predictably, some things changed by returning to the past. The same *Times* article touts the advantages of nearby ferries when traffic congestion peaks.

My mom rode the ferry to work in New York in the 1930s. Trolley lines drained commuters from all over Bergen County, carried them down the Palisades, and dropped them at the 125th Street ferry dock in Edgewater. From the corner of River Road and Dempsey Avenue, it was a short, straight shot across the Hudson to Manhattan. The ferry ran into the 1950s, and I remember riding it to New York with my mother to buy my Easter outfits at Best's. On the ferry, we could sit outside on benches in the cool wind, and I never got sick to my stomach like I did on Public Service buses.

Like many American towns and cities, Edgewater now

has a parrot flock, but I remember instead vast flocks of starlings flying west at dawn and back east at dusk when I was a child. They commuted from roosts under the West Side Highway to eat all day in the Meadowlands. The dawn flight posed no problem; their guts were empty. But my mother would run to pull her wash in as the evening flight began. A well-fed flock of starlings could send her clean laundry right back into the hamper.

And I remember the smell of industry in the 1950s—banana oil, coffee, linseed oil. The banana oil and roasting coffee smelled good, but I wouldn't miss the bitter smell of linseed oil today. Veterans Field was closed from 2011 until 2017 because contaminated concrete was used in some earlier reconstruction. The park has reopened and is well manicured; the ballfields are carpeted with plastic turf. In the 1950s, the park was where we ice-skated on a flooded basketball court and where I mooned over the boy wearing No. 8 at Little League games. Back then, the Veterans' Housing sat across River Road from the park. The attached, single-floor, one-family homes looked like the houses in my Monopoly set. They'd been built for vets after World War II and, in my childhood, also became the home of a family who'd fled the 1956 Hungarian Revolution. In the tiny houses' stead now is a condominium complex. I wonder if somewhere behind it there's still a shortcut up the rocks to Route 5?

* * *

I had lived away from town a long time when my friend Nora called me with surprising news. She'd been at a party in trendy Hoboken and heard someone mention the "Gold Coast" in New Jersey. She asked where that was, and the answer was "Edgewater." We'd both lived in and loved the old idiosyncratic, blue-collar Edgewater, and we had a laugh at "Gold Coast."

Later, I found online entries that named my blue-collar factory town among best places to live near New York to find the rich and single.

"And Geraldo Rivera parks a Bentley in his garage in the Camps," Claire said when I read them to her. She was living in the Idaho panhandle by then but still had family in town.

I wanted to see the change myself, so I visited. One of my schools was still open and full of life and noise. The other school had become a senior citizen center—also full of life, but with far less noise. (It's now a school again.) An apartment complex, not the Alcoa plant, surrounded the old Dutch cemetery. The big, black gates of the cemetery were locked, but a friend and I climbed over them. We found Go-won-go Mohawk's grave. Without the nearby heartbeat of the aluminum presses, the cemetery seemed abandoned, and we didn't stay long. A Persian restaurant sat where the Wanda Canoe Club used to be. Ingold's Garage was a Pilates studio. Whole Foods covered the site of the old Sugar House/Ford Plant. And where I'd sat as a kid having pizza and Pepsi with my parents in the Belle Ann Tavern, Pellegrino water was being sold.

Nothing wrong with any of that, but it's not for me. That's not my river town; mine lives in my memories now. Writing about it is how I visit.

The Edgewater Skyline Today

Photo by Marc Kaufman

PART FOUR
THE WIDE SEA

The Familiar Stranger

What had my father thought as he skated smoothly away from me on that iced basketball court on the shore of the Hudson? "You're not trying," was all he said. Was it so easy to learn how to skate backwards? I believed what he said about me—I was someone who didn't try-- and I felt the worse for that. And my mother? Did she feel torn between wanting me to stretch my wings and wanting to protect herself from the hurts I'd inevitably experience in the world? She pressed to keep me safe and near, and I saw myself as incompetent and a likely source of heartache. I felt the worse for that, too. Eventually I had children of my own and felt the vastness of my love for them and the terrifying vulnerability that love brought me. I learned how complicated it is to be responsible for another human being within the joy of that vast love and the terror of that vulnerability.

But I wanted my children to be strong and confident in ways I had not been. So I practiced not running to them as soon as they fell down. I let them do things that were just beyond what they seemed ready for. I bit my tongue when they took the risks they needed to take. And I tried to back them up when they were in over their heads. But I rarely felt that I knew what I was doing. And I fretted over my lost freedom. My sons were burdens. Then guilt would rush in. No, they were gifts I didn't deserve. They baffled me. And sometimes they seemed not to understand a word I said. They were from my body, but they could not know my thoughts, even when I tried hard to explain them. However, what we have always had is the trust that we love one other. We four occupy that love like a comfortable old couch, whether we understand what's going on among us or not.

My parents' love for me was also like that couch. While their behavior was sometimes mysterious, even hurtful, to me, I can still curl up in their love. And I hope they felt the same about my love for them. They're always with me, and the best parts of our relationship support my health and strength. I trust whatever story they would tell, if they could, of our life together, but they would not tell the same story I've told. Read this one as mine alone.

Whose River?

In the same vein, don't take as hard and fast fact what anybody writes or says about the Hudson River. Like love, the river is too old, too big, too strong to characterize, and it moves and changes and is never the same for any two people. What authenticity I claim for my stories, I claim through having lived with the river. And, like living with a person, what I say about that relationship comes through the filter of me. If my haunted dreams take place on the Hudson's shoreline, that's my story. If memories of joy and adventure take place on that same shoreline, that's my story, too.

Young on the River with My Mom and Dad
Author's Photo

I've read books about the Hudson by writers who sound certain of their claims, but I find their facts arguable. One book I read says that by 1960, from Albany to New York, the river was off-limits to swimmers and that people avoided eating fish from it. Maybe that's the historical record, but it's not *my* river experience. Although my father sold his outboard after Pearl Harbor because he knew he was headed to war, he replaced it in 1953. His new boat was from Canada, a beautiful mahogany speedboat with an inboard Chrysler Crown engine. He got back on the Hudson with us after I got Salk shots and a Polio Pioneer card in third grade. With polio out of the picture, my mother felt I was safe from the worst that river water could do to me.

I swam in the river every summer after. My dad would run the boat north past the Tappan Zee Bridge to Croton on the east bank. The crooked northern shore of Croton Point forms a pretty little bay there. The ocean tides don't come that far up from New York Harbor, so the water is fresh and cleaner. My dad would cut the boat engine, and the backwash would just be hitting the stern as I cannon-balled into the water. Starting in the late 1950s, I also swam off the boat just north of the George Washington Bridge on summer evenings. Hundreds of times swimming in the Hudson and only once did I pick up a germ. Lesson learned: Best not to go swimming with nicks all over your legs from shaving.

Riding on the Boat with My Dad

Author's Photo

Growing up in Edgewater during the 1950s and 1960s, I saw plenty of people eat Hudson River fish. In chill early April, lines of shad poles crossed the river. The poles were driven into the bottom muck to anchor nets underwater where shad swam north to spawn. When I walked out our front door, I smelled the Ingolds' smoking shed turning shad skin gold and infusing its flesh with the smoky scent of winter turning into spring.

In the 1950s, my dad and my grandfather spent long, cold weekend mornings on docks in Edgewater fishing for tommy cod. They used little rigs with jingle bells on them. To make the rigs, they drove the pointy ends of 8-inch metal rods into the wood of a dock and tied fishing line and the bells onto eyes at the top of the rods. Whenever a tommy cod hit, the little bell rang. In between hits, my dad and grandpa kept warm with homemade grappa. Wikipedia says that at that time those fish were already filling up with PCBs dumped into the river by General Electric. But this is my river story, and my dad and grandpa never got sick from those fish. They both died of cancers caused by tobacco. I hate the tobacco industry; it really is filthy.

Rowing Trophy Winner at Edgewater's Water Festival
Author's Photo

For me, the best creature in the river was *Callinectes sapidus*. Its name comes from the Greek words for "beautiful" and "swimmer" and from the Latin word for "savory." "Beautiful swimmer" is fine with me, but I'd change the second word to *dulcis* because there is nothing in this world sweeter to eat than a steamed blue claw crab fresh out of the Hudson River. Maybe animals that eat any old kind of garbage like pigs and crabs do taste extra sweet. My dad waved away any doubts about the safety of Hudson River crabs. "Crabs are self-cleaners," he'd say. "Perfectly safe to eat."

At the little boat club we belonged to, kids hung crab nets off docks and floats all summer. On incoming tides, we tossed a wire killifish pot from the dock. We gave the tiny fish a while to swim into holes at both ends of the cylindrical trap then harvested them. We strung these bait fish on the bottom of a one-foot wire cube that was the crab net and threw the cube into the river. When the net hit bottom, its four hinged sides fell open, and, with luck, hungry crabs trooped in to eat the killifish. (Crabs like raw chicken, too, but the mothers I knew didn't let us feed people food to crabs, except for the chicken necks.) Pulling up a crab net at the right time took some experience. Wait too long and both the fish and the crabs were gone. Pull too soon and the crabs hadn't gotten there yet. It was a rite of passage for a kid to grab a live crab for the first time and transfer it from a net to a bucket. Gripping it from behind in the middle of its body, we were safe from its waving claws.

As I promised him I would do, I spread my dad's ashes over his favorite crabbing spot in the river. His friend Richie rowed me out a ways off Veterans Field. The funeral home had given me his ashes in a container that looked like a shiny new paint can without a label. Richie and I were a little scared to see what was left of my father, but it was unremarkable gray grit. It looked like the ashes Claire's dad shoveled out of their coal furnace in the winter. Just me, my dad, Richie, and the river on a June afternoon—the peacefulness soothed my pain at losing him. Five years later, Richie rowed me out to scatter my mother's ashes, too. "When the time comes, put me with him," she said, so I did. A real Hudson River love story those two.

I'm not arguing that the Hudson wasn't dirty years ago. New York City flushed a lot of disgusting stuff into our part of the river. If we came up near a turd or a "Hudson River whitefish" when we were swimming, we scrambled fast in the opposite direction. The Scenic Hudson Preservation Conference v. Federal Power Commission suit, decided in 1965, accomplished wonders for the river and the environmental movement. But the Hudson wasn't a dead, deserted, unloved river before that first suit was filed.

"Until people start to love their river," Pete Seeger once said, "it's going to be a sewer." He made it sound as if no one loved the Hudson River before the *Clearwater* came along. Well, in Edgewater, we loved it. We swam in it and, if we weren't careful, swallowed some of it when we jumped in. We disobeyed our parents and prowled its banks. We ate out of it.

We zoomed across its surface. We watched it under blue skies and in quiet snowfalls and through hurricanes. We walked along it in deep winter and heard floating ice sheets squeal against each other. Some of us dreamed deeply about it and learned who we were. Some of us left our parents in it. We loved it all right.

Even now I look at the Hudson River and feel it's mine. Why this sense of personal ownership? My father gave me the river. Once a friend asked about what I was writing here, and my vague mention of my father and the river wasn't clear. "Did he work on the river?" the friend asked. No, I said, his connection with the river was deeper than work. He loved it. It had held him, cooled him, frightened him, filled him with joy at its beauty, set his imagination sailing, and taught him to exercise good sense and to watch and listen in patient silence.

We Loved It

Author's Photo

The river presses sense memories into the people who love it. It leaves a certain smell on swimmers, a nice smell, not a bad one; it stayed on my skin even after my clothes were back on. And even on the hottest New Jersey nights, the river kept me cool for hours after a dip. On the shore of the Hudson, my dad let me stroke the fur of baby shrews he found in a nest tucked under a boulder. He made me smell the cucumber scent of a copperhead snake he'd killed when the snake just wouldn't stay out of a path we used. I felt the clammy fear that could erupt in an emergency on the river. Riding south one evening after a day in Interstate Park, we saw two dots midstream turn into men's heads as we got closer. We stopped for them, and I saw the white-knuckled panic in the grip each man clamped on my father's arms as he lifted them into our boat. They were just young guys who had walked over the bridge from New York and thought they could swim back to the city. Their faces, white as fish bellies, showed how close they'd felt to drowning.

"You have to respect the water," my father told me over and over. While he was foolish enough to drive his car sometimes after drinking, he was never drunk when he drove his boat.

In his 14-foot runabout, my father courted the woman he married, a city girl who didn't know port from starboard. She was big, taller than he was, and when the outboard motor bit in and the front of the boat shot up, he taught her to flop onto the covered prow to bring it back down. And he expected her to be quick about it. They spent lazy Sundays on the riverbank in Palisades Interstate Park, eating sandwiches and reading newspapers, far away from their five-and-a-half-day workweek to come. I wonder if my parents shared slow, delicious kisses on the riverbank in those summers like I did in mine.

My Dad

My Mom

Author's Photos

Along the Shore

My father declared the Hudson "the most beautiful river in the world" and he had seen quite a few. It was his river and he knew why he loved it. Riding the currents of what I grew into on the banks of the Hudson, I've seen quite a few rivers, too, although none spoke to me the way my river does. I've stood on the banks of the Avon and the Thames, of the Delaware and the Middle Fork of the Salmon, of the Seine and the Arno, of the Chao Phraya and the Yamuna—each like a huge animal, a living thing with its unique way of being.

Moving water takes us to new places. It tells us stories as it runs against the still land. Its forces—sometimes opposed, sometimes mingled--speak to us of life.

Land~Water   Stillness~Motion   Solid~Fluid

Awake~Asleep   Conscious~Unconscious

Fact~Memory   Objective~Subjective

Parent~Child   Lover~Beloved

What is a dream if we're never awake to consider it? What is a fact without memory to give it meaning? What are our parents without children? Imagine a world of restless motion only. Imagine a world of profound stillness only. Imagine a world without shorelines. Nothing happens. There are no stories to tell.

Acknowledgements

Even a memoir centered on one person's evolving perceptions results from many people's contributions. Mine is no exception. I am indebted to my mother and my father for sharing with me their love of Edgewater, the Hudson River, story telling, and writing; to my first readers, Lea Chartock and Marc Kaufman, who got my rough draft on the right path; to my editor at Serving House Books, Walter Cummins, who immediately understood what I was trying to do and helped me do it better; to Carolyn Carr for the generous gift of her photos and permission to use them; to Ross Chapple, photo-tech master extraordinaire; to my friends (you know who you are) and to my family, especially David, John, Beth, and Miles, who fill my life with intelligence, laughter, and enthusiasm; and to all the wonderful characters I grew up among in Edgewater.

I want to thank the many writers who gave me permission to quote their words as I told my story.

I also want to acknowledge three publications that, though only one is quoted in this book, provided me with orienting information and with platforms from which to imagine stories:

> *A History of the Borough of Edgewater: Centennial Edition 1894-1994,* by Lynn Fox, published by the Borough of Edgewater, 1994
>
> *Images of America: Edgewater,* by Douglas E. Hall with the Edgewater Cultural and Historical Committee, published by Arcadia Publishing, 2005
>
> *Edgewater Historical Survey,* Works Progress Administration, Project #693, 1936

Flights of fancy and any mistakes herein are my responsibility.